Intermediate Sanctions: Sentencing in the 1990s

Edited by

John Ortiz Smykla
University of Alabama

William L. Selke
Indiana University

ACJS Series Editor, Dean J. Champion

Academy of Criminal Justice Sciences
Northern Kentucky University
402 Nunn Hall
Highland Heights, KY 41076

Anderson Publishing Co.
Criminal Justice/Paralegal Division
P.O. Box 1576
Cincinnati, OH 45201-1576

Intermediate Sanctions:
Sentencing in the 1990s

Copyright © 1995 by Anderson Publishing Co. and
Academy of Criminal Justice Sciences

 The text of this book is printed on recycled paper.

ISBN 0-87084-825-9

Library of Congress Catalog Number 94-71862

Gail Eccleston *Editor*   *Managing Editor* Kelly Humble

Cover photograph by
Tim Grondin/PhotoDesign

Preface

It is more than a pleasure to launch my editorship of the ACJS/Anderson Monograph Series on *Issues in Crime and Justice* with a volume dedicated to an examination of intermediate punishments. John Smykla and Bill Selke have assembled an admirable collection of essays of theory and research about a most timely topic. The addition of this volume to the series is both needed and welcomed.

 Corrections in the United States is in grave trouble. Currently, most prison and jail systems are overcrowded in one way or another, whether the measures are in terms of inmates per square feet of space, inmates relative to the number of beds, or inmates relative to original design capacities of incarcerative facilities. As President Bill Clinton successfully markets legislation in the form of a massive anti-crime bill, one important outcome will be to drive prison and jail inmate populations upward. A substantial proportion of prisons and jails are under court order to reduce inmate overcrowding. Despite large-scale prison and jail construction projects under way in numerous jurisdictions, accommodating the convicted offender population currently *not* incarcerated would require four to five times as much prison and jail space than presently exists. And this unrealistic step would only match *current* offender numbers. When three-time recidivists are factored into the inmate population equation with mandatory life sentences, the numbers of permanent jail and prison occupants will escalate dramatically. We can anticipate, therefore, that within a year or two, new alternative arrangements for supervising these growing offender aggregates will have to be devised. Or existing management solutions will be expanded to encompass low-risk, nonviolent property offenders, or those least likely to pose societal risk.

 Whether we agree or disagree, jail and prison are not necessary for all convicted offenders. Some persons believe that *all* convicted offenders should do the statutory time for their offending as a punishment. These same persons do not equate anything *less* than flat time served in a jail or prison with *punishment* in the true sense of the word. Thus, home incarceration, electronic monitoring, "smart sentencing," "creative sentencing," victim compensation or restitution, and more intensive supervised probation would not pass muster as true punishments. There are several problems with this view. First, it is logistically impossible to lock up everyone currently convicted of a crime and in need of incarceration. There is simply not enough space to house *all* convicted offenders. We are having trouble accommodating only about 20 percent of them presently. A second problem is the general failure to regard intermediate punishment solutions as punishment. Critics of intermediate punishment do not accept the contention that these forms of client/offender supervision are *continuations of punishment.* A third problem is that many nonviolent, nonserious offenders are first-time offenders. Many of these persons will *never reoffend.* Thus, incarcerating them is likely a waste of valuable jail and prison space, where more serious and dangerous offenders could and should be accommodated instead.

Jailing or imprisoning convicted offenders is also expensive. Per diem inmate maintenance costs vary from $15 per inmate per day in some jurisdictions to nearly $100 per inmate per day in other jurisdictions. Actual jail or prison construction is also prohibitive. Considering the initial costs of building a single cell, these costs vary from $25,000 per inmate to perhaps $75,000 or more per inmate. Increasingly scarce resources, greater taxation for more people, and rising interest rates, together with the fact that corrections is a low-priority funding consideration in city, county, state, and national budgets, means that it is unlikely that we will *ever* be able to construct *sufficient* inmate space. There will always be jail and prison overcrowding, and much of this overcrowding will be chronic.

An intelligent and practical response within the correctional community to deal with the overcrowding problem is to establish intermediate punishments, where the costs of supervising offenders are only a fraction of the costs of incarcerating them. Furthermore, there is merit in the argument that these intermediate punishments offer client/offenders opportunities to remain within or become integrated into their communities as useful, productive, and law-abiding citizens. It is true that a portion of these client/offenders recidivate. However, many intermediate punishment programs show great promise because of a significant reduction in client/offender recidivism. Compared with parolees or standard probationers with little or no supervision and personal responsibility, client/offenders within different kinds of intermediate punishment programs tend to have substantially lower rates of recidivism, controlling for prior records, race/ethnicity, socioeconomic status, gender, and instant offenses. No client/offender supervision program is perfect. Yet, intermediate punishment programs offer relatively low rates of recidivism at less cost to taxpayers compared with the cost of incarcerating them.

One savings accruing from these intermediate punishment programs is labor. Since almost every intermediate punishment program is integrated into community corrections, there is growing use made of paraprofessionals and volunteers. While these persons are not necessarily skilled therapists who can work with offenders, they do offer other skills that permit full-time personnel to apply their own training and abilities more strategically. Volunteers assist client/offenders in filling out employment applications, and they assist in networking among various community agencies and services. In a time of scarce resources, intermediate punishments are economical, and program quality is not necessarily compromised.

This volume explores existing intermediate punishment programs and their success potential. These editors have provided a rich array of contributors who delve into many issues relative to intermediate punishments. The editors also offer projections about the future of intermediate punishments as we move closer to the year 2000. Intermediate punishments may be viewed as punitive, to be sure. But we must not neglect the reintegrative and rehabilitative potential of such programs, provided that the right types of client/offenders are targeted. Program success rates are highly dependent upon quality control. Not all convicted offenders are suited for intermediate punishment programs. When client/offenders recidivate when enrolled in such programs, a significant proportion of these "failures" never should have been included in them in the first place. Many jurisdictions rely on prediction measures to make dangerousness forecasts. These forecasts are less than perfect. Scale scores may indicate that certain types of persons are or will be dangerous if released within their communities. However, these persons may never commit new offenses or pose a danger to anyone. These are called *false positives*. In a sense, we do such persons an *injustice* when we incarcerate them, sometimes for lengthy terms. Other client/offenders are released in their communities under loose supervision, when dangerousness indices declare them to be safe. Some of them turn out *not* to be safe, and, while free, they injure or kill innocent victims. Parole boards and judges fear making decisions about such offenders, because they can deceive our instrumentation and behave in ways contrary to our predictions.

Client/offenders eligible for intermediate punishment programs are those who indicate strong rehabilitative potential. It is difficult for any of us to know for sure who these offenders are. We do the best we can with our state-of-the-art instrumentation and make the best of an uncomfortable situation. Only the test of time will tell us whether we are on the right track concerning the use of intermediate punishments. I happen to think that these intermediate punishment programs are the way of our correctional future. We are currently in a learning phase. We are learning about those client/offender characteristics that are most closely associated with success measures in intermediate punishment programs. We are also learning much about those who fail in such programs. Our instrumentation is becoming more sophisticated, although we must never lose sight of the fact that more simple assessments of risk and dangerousness may be better than complex ones.

The selection of chapter contributions is sufficiently broad so that every reader having an interest in intermediate punishments will derive some value from chapter contents. As you read this work, you are on the cutting edge of community corrections for the 1990s.

Dean J. Champion
ACJS/Anderson Monograph Series Editor
Minot State University

Acknowledgments

There is no more current research on intermediate sanctions than the 10 articles published here. The concept for this volume was suggested several years ago by our friend and 1992–93 ACJS President, Bob Bohm. One of the editors (JOS) was a member of the 1993 ACJS Program Committee and received over 90 abstracts in the general area of punishment and corrections. One-fourth of these focused on intermediate sanctions and all but one agreed to write simultaneously for the conference and this volume. There could have been no better preparation for a volume of current research.

At the meeting in Kansas City, both editors attended the sessions where these papers were first presented. We asked questions, as did the other participants, and found ourselves in the most fortunate position of hearing our colleagues who attended these sessions offer valuable discussion and critique of the papers. Whether or not they knew it, they acted as informal referees. Contributors were asked to consider the comments offered at the annual meeting before submitting final copies to the editors. We proceeded then with a round of formal reviews and selected these 10 papers. Had there been no space limitations, all 23 would have made an excellent volume. So that we could publish this volume as *current* research, authors revised and returned their manuscripts in stellar time. No editors could have been more fortunate.

The 19 authors of these 10 papers offer us many years of academic and applied experience and some new beginnings. Some of the authors are well-known while others are just starting their professional careers. Together their research will help policymakers, correctional managers, and students to better understand the theoretical and policy issues of intermediate sanctions.

Without the advice and support of Dean Champion, ACJS/Anderson Monograph Series Editor, all of our energy might have been in vain. Dean helped us move carefully and swiftly across this project. Throughout the year he advised us by phone, letter, fax, and a meeting in Kansas City. Any advice he gave us that could have improved this volume but which we ignored is our fault.

And finally, we acknowledge the support our universities and families gave us in the preparation of this volume.

Contents

Introduction:
Toward a More Comprehensive
Model of Sentencing

William L. Selke
Indiana University

John Ortiz Smykla
University of Alabama

Sentencing criminal offenders has become complex. The sentencing decision used to be fairly simple because there were limited options. Today, there are many more sanctions available to trial court judges. They are no longer forced to choose between traditional imprisonment and routine probation. During the last three decades, several new sentencing alternatives emerged. Judges in most jurisdictions may now choose from a range of sanctions that include fines, restitution, community service, residential programs such as work release and halfway houses, and nonresidential programs involving drug and alcohol treatment, as well as other types of counseling and therapy. These sentencing alternatives have already received a great deal of attention in the literature and will not be considered in this book. *Intermediate Sanctions: Sentencing in the 1990s* will examine three of the newest sanctions that move us toward a more systematic and comprehensive approach to sentencing in the criminal justice system.

Intermediate sanction is defined as a sentencing option that falls on a continuum between probation and prison. This book is devoted to describing and analyzing three of the most popular intermediate sanctions—boot camps, intensive supervision, and electronic monitoring. Each chapter presents discussions on the philosophies, practices, and evaluations or issues that are central to the continued development of community corrections. Most innovative community programs in corrections are conceived as enhancements to the traditional probation process and the programs mentioned above are not exceptions. These kinds of sentencing options have begun to provide trial court judges with more flexibility at the time sentences are handed down. However, difficult issues remain as to whether these programs are serving as alternatives to incarceration *OR* whether they have only widened the net to apply more restrictive measures to larger groups of offenders? There is also interest in the process through which offenders are selected for the various sentencing options, as well as the levels of success and failure for the new programs in terms of reducing rates of recidivism.

We believe the following collection of papers provides a stimulating and diverse examination of the most recent developments in the field of community corrections. Included are analyses of programs from New York to California and North Dakota to Florida. Some of the authors are academic researchers, others are practitioners who have been responsible for creating and implementing the new community programs. Readers will also find an interesting combination of sophisticated empirical studies along with commentary that proposes theoretical, conceptual, and organizational matters to be considered in the planning of future programs. We hope that you will find the volume informative and helpful in thinking about the continued evolution of community corrections.

The first section of papers deals with electronic monitoring. Electronic monitoring (EM) has rapidly become one of the most widespread and controversial innovations in community corrections since Schwitzgebel first introduced the idea in 1969. Monitoring equipment has become much more sophisticated with voice and visual validation, and the view from most quarters is that the equipment has evolved to a point where it is fairly reliable and consistent. A second major reason for the growing popularity of EM is that it usually pays for itself, often generating significant profits and seldom requiring a large initial investment of public funds. In addition, with its emphasis on surveillance and public safety, the EM concept has dovetailed with the increasingly punitive changes in social and legal ideologies over the past decade. Electronic monitoring has also been widely accepted because it helps to fill the gap between incarceration and simple probation. Intermediate sanctions are deemed worthwhile and necessary given the national crises of prison and jail overcrowding.

The widespread adoption of electronic monitoring has become controversial for several reasons. For many, it raises the specter of government as "Big Brother" spying on citizens with highly sophisticated electronic equipment that is not totally understood. Constitutional questions are raised regarding matters such as right to privacy, the Fifth Amendment privilege against self-incrimination, and equality of treatment under the law. Concerns are also being voiced with respect to the omnipresent issue of discretion in the criminal justice system. There are currently no national standards and few consistent guidelines for structuring the major decisions about who will be placed in

EM programs, how long they will be monitored, what kind of monitoring will be used, when will revocation proceedings be initiated, what will constitute successful completion of the program, and how successful are various methods of EM compared with traditional probation. Finally, there is the overriding debate about whether EM and other innovative community correctional programs are serving as alternatives to jail and prison sentences, or whether they are merely "widening the net" as is often claimed. The chapters in the following section address many of these issues. The authors have attempted to clarify the meaning and implementation of EM programs, and they have demonstrated the necessity for more systematic and meaningful evaluations.

In Chapter 1, Sheldon X. Zhang, Robert Polakow, and Barry J. Nidorf present an excellent overview of the many different ways in which electronic monitoring may be used within the justice system. Monitoring began and has generally been integrated within the correctional system as a condition for those placed on probation. However, this chapter makes it clear that EM can be used in a number of other ways as well. For example, there is discussion of the Supervised Release Program in which those who are unable to make bail and who do not qualify for release on recognizance are placed in electronically monitored home detention instead. At the other end of the system, they describe a program (The Work Furlough Electronic Home Detention Program) which allows those already sentenced to jail to work during the day and return home on electronic monitoring at night. The authors also discuss some of the potential problems in working through bureaucratic barriers to initiate programs, and they describe the procedures that are used to select and monitor private vendors who are contracted to provide monitoring services.

Sudipto Roy and Michael P. Brown, in Chapter 2, present one of the better evaluations of an electronic monitoring program. The authors used a quasi-experimental design to compare the relative effects of an electronic monitoring home detention program and the more traditional manual form of supervising juveniles in home detention through random home visits. In this research, the electronic monitoring group was compared with a matched sample of juveniles under manual supervision in terms of program completion rates and post-program recidivism. It was found that the electronic monitoring group had higher rates of successful program completion, as well as lower rates of recidivism following home detention, in comparison with the manual supervision group. Although there was an attempt to match the two groups, the findings from this study must be reviewed with some caution since there were larger percentages of felony offenders, repeat offenders, and offenders with substance abuse records in the manual supervision program. This piece of research clearly illustrates the need for continued attention to the selection process in the placement of offenders into EM programs and the benefits of using more sophisticated evaluation designs in the assessment of program effects, regardless of the particular program.

The final chapter in Section I is another contribution by Brown and Roy on an evaluation of electronic monitoring with adults in Utica, New York. In addition to comparing the rates of successful completion in electronic and manual monitoring programs, the authors attempt to determine which variables are most closely associated with success or failure under either type of supervision. They conclude that certain individual, social, and case characteristics are good predictors of failure depending on whether electronic or manual supervision is used. This research also contains some interesting findings with regard to the effects of the length of time offenders are exposed to the different methods of supervision.

Section II examines issues in boot camp. Boot camps, sometimes called shock incarceration programs, have grown in popularity almost as rapidly as electronic monitoring programs. The reasons are probably similar. Boot camps, like electronic monitoring, conjured up images that were highly consistent with the conservatism of the 1980s. Similar to monitoring, the boot camp concept was aimed at modifying individual behaviors by using tougher and more intense correctional methods. While EM attempted to bring about these changes through more intense surveillance, boot camps hoped to change offenders by making their supervision and training more intense. Many of the same issues related to monitoring have been raised with respect to boot camps. The next two chapters offer insights into the nature of boot camp programs and the potential effectiveness of this concept as part of the new intermediate sanction schemata.

Chapter 4 is a multi-state evaluation of boot camps by Claire Souryal and Doris Layton MacKenzie. Through the use of survival analysis procedures, the researchers compare recidivism outcomes for graduates and dropouts from shock incarceration programs with those of probationers and prison parolees in Georgia, Florida, South Carolina, and Louisiana. While the results of this study offer limited support for the effectiveness of boot camp programs, the authors are prudent in pointing out some of the thorny issues that complicate this type of research. For example, the need for true experimental designs and random assignment is made clear because of the voiced concerns regarding selection biases and unequivalent comparison groups. Other insightful comments are made with respect to the manner in which levels of supervision can effect recidivism rates regardless of the impact of specific programs.

In Chapter 5, Laura A. Gransky, Thomas C. Castellano, and Ernest L. Cowles discuss the findings of a national survey to determine the goals and activities in a broad range of shock incarceration/boot camp programs. The survey obtained information and attitudes from officials in departments of corrections, program administrators, and treatment personnel about the boot camps that they operate. Results from this study show that the primary emphasis in most boot camp programs is on physical training, drill, and ceremony, although some consideration has recently been given to various treatment methods including alcohol and drug treatment and education. Interestingly, there do appear to be differences in perceptions among the different groups who have responsibilities for developing and implementing boot camp programs.

Section III focuses on intensive probation supervision. Sometimes viewed as enhancements to traditional probation and other times designed to be an alternative to incarceration, this intermediate sanction has also attracted a great deal of attention and debate. IPS raises a number of interesting theoretical and programmatic questions. For example, do smaller caseloads for probation officers result in more effective supervision, or is there a higher rate of technical violations given the more rigorous supervision practices? Furthermore, there are a variety of unresolved policy issues such as the selection of offenders for IPS and the appropriate activities for IPS officers. The two articles in this section offer a wealth of information about the intensive supervision option.

In Chapter 6, Betsy Fulton and Susan Stone develop a broad-ranging and innovative proposal for redesigning intensive supervision programs. IPSs have come to play an important role in our attempts to address problems of prison crowding and the paucity of community correctional alternatives. As research associates for the American Probation and Parole Association, the authors focus on a number of the most perplexing questions regarding the nature and effectiveness of intensive supervision programs, as well as other newly developed intermediate sanctions. They provide thoughtful insights into the philosophies and practices of IPSs as they have evolved during a period that has been characterized as more punitive and less oriented toward treatment and rehabilitation. The proposal outlined in this piece suggests that IPSs can become more rehabilitative, and perhaps more effective, with some modifications in the conceptual framework and the incorporation of certain novel program elements.

In Chapter 7, John T. Whitehead, Larry S. Miller, and Laura B. Myers use discriminant analysis to determine the characteristics of prison and jail inmates, regular probationers, and offenders sentenced to the intermediate sanctions of intensive supervision and community corrections. Once they identify the characteristics, they address the related issues of diversion and net widening by evaluating the rates at which prison-bound and probation-bound offenders are sentenced to the intermediate sanctions. Their data from the State of Tennessee illustrates the engaging and perplexing nature of this field of research. There is some evidence that the intermediate sanctions are sometimes used for those who were likely to have been incarcerated. There is also some indication than many of those who would have been expected to receive regular probation were sentenced to the more restrictive intermediate sanctions. A number of suggestions are offered with respect to future research in this area, and thoughtful comments are presented on systematizing and improving the sentencing process.

In the final chapter of Section III, Stephen Haas and Edward J. Latessa present an analysis of a special probation program as it functions within a small rural setting. The authors compare an intensive supervision caseload with a group of offenders placed on regular probation. One important conclusion was that the group under intensive supervision did have more serious criminal histories, suggesting that the new program was being utilized for those most in need. Interestingly, however, it was discovered that the groups were not significantly different in terms of recidivism. Although the intensively supervised group had more technical violations of their probation conditions, both groups had similarly high rates of success in avoiding further arrests and convictions. This piece also offers an insightful analysis of the variables that are related to a successful completion of probation.

In Section IV, we have included two papers that address a range of important issues that continue to emerge in the field of community corrections. The first eight chapters indicate that innovative programs are being developed at a breakneck pace without adequate concern for some of the conceptual and operational matters that will determine the eventual success or failure of the programs. The goals of corrections continue to be so intertwined and overlapping that it is difficult to assess the effectiveness of various sanctions. The community has not often been truly involved in planning, implementing, and evaluating new problems. And the widespread concern over the issue of race is a matter that continues to hamper enthusiasm for many innovative program ideas. These matters, and more, are illuminated within the papers of the final section of the book.

Involvement of the community in "community corrections" might seem to be a given. It is not, however. As Stone and Fulton note in their chapter, more attention is needed to involve the community in local correctional efforts. Such attention is forthcoming in Chapter 9 by Paige H. Ralph, Richard M. Hoekstra, and Timothy R. Brehm who consider this matter within the context of the rural community. The authors describe the unique problems that face sparsely populated states like North Dakota as they attempt to develop community corrections programs. Offenders are dispersed widely across the state, local and state resources are limited, and there are only small numbers of correctional workers throughout the state. Ralph, Hoekstra, and Brehm present a thought-provoking essay that will be of particular interest to correctional workers in all rural areas. They emphasize the importance of community corrections boards to stimulate the development of innovative programs for offenders. They also review several of the community programs that have been designed for the unique circumstances of the small, rural state.

As earlier chapters illustrated (e.g., Brown & Roy), the issue of race continues to be a major concern in the implementation of new sentencing options. There has been much concern that minorities are more likely to be placed in programs that increase the level of punishment and less likely to be included in those that are less punitive in nature. In Chapter 10, Paul C. Friday and Robert A. Wertkin discover that race also plays an important role in the successful completion of a residential probation center program. This relatively uncommon probation center concept was found to have a high rate of success in terms of future recidivism, although the positive findings were tempered by the fact that nonwhites had lower rates of successful program completion, which was a factor that was significantly related to recidivism. The authors provide a valuable description of the program elements in the probation center, and they offer useful comments regarding the future development of residential probation centers as another of the new intermediate sanctions.

This collection of writings demonstrates both the hopes that are offered by the newer intermediate sanctions and the fears that accompany the development of innovative sentencing alternatives. There are many issues yet to be resolved. It is not clear yet that the intermediate sanctions are being used for those who would have received harsher sentences. Questions still exist about the overall effectiveness of intermediate sanctions in reducing recidivism. The goals of various sanctions and the activities within particular kinds of programs are still evolving. Plans for using multiple sanctions in combination are not forthcoming. And whether intermediate sanctions will alleviate prison and jail overcrowding is a critical issue still open to debate. Nevertheless, even with these unresolved issues, the continued profusion of intermediate sanctions is filling the void between probation and prison. It is now becoming necessary for us to conceptualize how a more robust sentencing model can be best used to achieve greater equity in the justice system and tranquility in society.

The authors and editors of *Intermediate Sanctions: Sentencing in the 1990s* hope that the reader will find some thoughts and ideas throughout these pages that might stimulate thinking about potential refinements in the sentencing process. A more effective system of justice will require an approach to sentencing that entails both a comprehensive series of calibrated sanctions and a detailed set of guidelines for making prudent use of the expanded model. The sentencing decision is the fulcrum upon which our system of justice attempts to balance the desire for public safety and the protection of individual liberties. For researchers, practitioners, and policymakers in the field of criminal justice, the writings that follow offer an abundance of new information about three innovative, albeit, controversial intermediate sanctions. Sentencing in the 1990s is likely to become still more complex and sophisticated. Such changes will be less tumultuous and more effective as we come to better understand the concept of intermediate sanctions. May these materials make some small contribution toward this goal.

Section I

ELECTRONIC MONITORING

In the following section, the topic of discussion is electronic monitoring, one of the most sophisticated and controversial of a new genre of community correctional alternatives collectively known as intermediate sanctions. The criminal justice system has been profoundly influenced in recent years by various technological advancements. Police departments have benefited from advances in criminalistics and the computerization of crime statistics. Criminal courts have become more efficient through the use of management information systems and automated scheduling programs. Jails and prisons have continued to make use of innovative security and surveillance equipment. However, it has only been very recently that the field of community corrections has incorporated some of the newer technologies.

Electronic monitoring (EM) is the most interesting innovation in community corrections in some time. It has created an entirely new intermediate sanction that has become widely used and fiercely debated. EM used in conjunction with house arrest has several appealing features. It makes use of cutting edge technology. When used carefully, it can be a very effective approach to supervising offenders in the community. EM contains a punitive element. Few people savor the thought of wearing an unremovable anklet that allows someone to monitor their whereabouts at all times. Monitoring and house arrest are very inexpensive sanctions when compared to incarceration. And most importantly, the concept of electronic monitoring is marketable. EM programs hold an appeal for judges and politicians, probation officials, the media, and the public alike. It is one of the few community sentencing options that has not been subjected to vitriolic criticisms as being "soft on crime" and a threat to public safety.

What makes monitoring even more interesting is that it has the potential to alleviate the most pressing problem in the justice system, namely, prison and jail overcrowding. For the large percentage of offenders who are found guilty of nonviolent crimes, EM is a viable sentencing option. We have already seen that judges are willing to use this intermediate sanction as an alternative to imprisonment, and the public has thus far been accepting of the notion of house arrest with monitoring. But there are still certain issues that remain unresolved.

The first three chapters of this book address the most recent questions that have been raised regarding EM. These materials contain informative descriptions of actual monitoring programs and present analyses that begin to clarify the essential operational elements in EM programming. We will learn more about the philosophies and the day-to-day operations of monitoring programs. In addition, we will be given data that allows us to make judgments as to the effects, both positive and negative, of such programs. While there should be no rush to judgment, it is important to understand the implementation and evaluation of major monitoring programs. Some changes will, of course, be necessary. Modifications will be made as we begin to learn more about matters such as who should be placed in EM programs, how the sanction should be applied (e.g., length of time on EM and intensity of surveillance), and what is to happen in the case of failure.

While this section does not hold the answers to all the concerns, there is a wealth of information that should prove useful in our further considerations of intermediate sanctions generally and electronic monitoring in particular. Trial court judges continue to search for meaningful options for use with younger, soft core, nonviolent offenders. The overcrowding crises in our jails and prisons forces judges, legislators, and other officials to search for viable alternatives. In these chapters, it will be seen that electronic monitoring may be one of the alternatives that has become a feasible community correctional option.

1

Varied Uses of Electronic Monitoring: The Los Angeles County Experience*

Sheldon X. Zhang
California State University at San Marcos

Robert Polakow
Los Angeles County Probation Department

Barry J. Nidorf
Los Angeles County Probation Department

BACKGROUND

Electronic monitoring (EM) arrived amidst a feverish effort in the criminal justice and corrections fields across the nation to search for punitive and safe alternatives or intermediate sanctions to alleviate jail and prison crowding.

Over the last 20 years, increasing crime rates, especially rates of violent offenses, have propelled the public to shift from the idea of rehabilitation, to call instead for "tough" approaches to criminals. Legislators responded to the popular sentiment by initiating a series of changes in policies ranging from mandatory sentences to longer incarceration (Morris & Tonry, 1990). By 1990, virtually all new sentencing law was designed to increase the certainty and length of prison terms, to incapacitate the active criminal, and to deter the rest (NCCD, 1992).

---

*Points of view are those of the authors and do not necessarily represent the position of the Los Angeles County Probation Department.

The effects of the policy change are apparent and drastic. As early as 1983, criminal justice administrators identified prison and jail crowding as the most important issue facing them (Gettinger, 1983). Prison populations have skyrocketed to the point where most jurisdictions across the country are desperate to find solutions (Fyfe, 1991; Jolin & Stipak, 1992). From 1970 to 1990, jail and prison populations increased by nearly four times (NCCD, 1992). By 1990, there were more than 1.1 million offenders in jail and prison (U.S. Department of Justice, 1992). The situation in probation and parole is even worse. By 1990, one out of every 46 adult Americans was under some form of correctional supervision. This is twice the rate of correctional control that existed in 1980, and nearly three times the level in 1974 (NCCD, 1992).

Los Angeles County experienced the same changes. In the past 10 years, the number of offenders held in the county jail more than doubled, and so did the probation population. Community corrections is no longer just for petty offenders or misdemeanants; increasingly, convicted felons are released early or are placed directly on probation due to jail crowding. In Los Angeles, 10 percent of the probation population are violent offenders and more than one-third are felony offenders.

As the nation's largest probation agency, Los Angeles County Probation Department currently supervises 90,000 adult offenders and 21,000 juvenile delinquents. They make up 42 percent of the state's probation population. The rapid growth of the offender population has clearly overwhelmed the agency's workforce, which is actually shrinking, and severely limited its capability to provide effective supervision. A large number of adult probationers are placed on automated "bank caseloads"—a computerized case management system that contacts offenders through correspondence and provides little actual supervision. The regular caseload size has reached 300 per officer. Probation officers oftentimes find themselves catching up with court-mandated paper-work rather than carrying out supervision activities. Probation in many cases ceases to function as a punishment. Searching for creative solutions to cope with the changing population with the least negative fiscal impact has become a pressing priority.

ELECTRONIC MONITORING IN INTENSIVE SUPERVISION

Historically, the justice system has had two options in dealing with convicted offenders—incarceration or probation. Both have been used excessively, with few intermediate sanctions in between (Morris & Tonry, 1990). With the exploding correctional population and prison crowding, a wave of noncustodial sanctions swept through the country including such alternatives as intensive supervision, shock incarceration, and house arrest (with and without an electronic monitoring component) (Byrne, 1990).

As the central component of these intermediate sanctions, intensive probation supervision (IPS) has been widely implemented as a community-based alternative (Petersilia & Turner, 1990; Byrne, 1990). IPS is designed primarily to reduce prison crowding and place more restrictions upon those prison-bound offenders who would otherwise receive routine probation, which in the current situation is little more than a suspended sentence or unsupervised community release.

Electronic monitoring arrived on the alternatives scene mostly as an enhancement to IPS. EM in and of itself is not a sanction, but a means of ensuring compliance with a curfew order or home detention. Since judicially approved electronic monitoring first appeared in 1983 in New Mexico, EM has received increasing interest and acceptance as an option for probation supervision across the country (Jolin & Stipak, 1992). By 1990, all 50 states had some EM programs and the offenders being monitored reached more than 12,000 in total (Renzema & Skelton, 1991). There are mainly two reasons for the rapid growth in EM. First, the justice system's frantic search for alternatives to incarceration has created a market of sufficient incentives for advances in electronic monitoring technology. Second, entrepreneurs have been quick in cashing in on this opportunity to pitch aggressive sales on this supposedly foolproof, safe, punitive, and cheap solution.

Research has been scarce and the numbers monitored are few. Of the limited articles, most are descriptive and lack a clear demonstration of what the program purports to accomplish—recidivism reduction (Vaughn, 1989; Mair, 1991; Renzema, 1991; Petersilia & Turner, 1990; Nellis, 1991). The number of offenders handled by any given program is usually too small to make a significant impact on correctional population. Despite initial problems, electronic monitoring continued to gain steady acceptance among the public and policymakers as a viable intermediate sanction which does not endanger public safety (Mair, 1991; Petersilia & Turner, 1990; Rogers & Jolin, 1989).

There has been little discussion in the existing literature about the theoretical basis of electronic monitoring. The growth and spread of electronic monitoring is occurring in the absence of reliable information about the effectiveness and impact of such programs (Maxfield & Baumer, 1990). It is primarily driven by the hard fact of prison crowding and the public concerns over community safety and punishment for offenders. In fact, this has been one of the few occasions in the history of criminal justice where policymakers and practitioners initiated experiments with new sanctions without much guidance from social scientists.

However, the use of EM is not without theoretical foundation. By attaching to the physical body, the electronic device constantly reminds the offender of his/her status and voices the warning that "someone is watching." This sentencing model clearly connotes the idea of specific deterrence that advocates for IPS have argued. From the classical perspective, criminals are thought to commit a crime when they determine that the benefits outweigh the pain of potential punishment. When the certainty of detection and punishment increases, propensity for criminal conduct decreases. EM is supposed to accomplish this by increasing the anxiety and apprehensiveness involved in committing a crime.

Close supervision, coupled with the threat of quick revocation and incarceration, is expected to increase offenders' awareness of the justice system's ability to detect and punish criminal behavior (Petersilia & Turner, 1990). EM certainly has enhanced the core component of probation supervision to an unprecedented level.

Although EM carries a clear deterrence undertone that emphasizes surveillance and incapacitation, there has been ethnographic evidence of its many rehabilitative potential. EM confines offenders in their own home environment and therefore does not subject them to the criminogenic influences of a jail or prison. It is a far less criminalizing sentencing option than imprisonment (Glaser & Watts, 1992b).

By maintaining family ties, employment or schooling, EM causes minimal disruption in the offender's routine daily life. For the unemployed offenders, EM allows them access to conventional rehabilitative activities such as job training and counseling (Jolin & Stipak, 1992). Most important of all, offenders can keep their jobs and pay taxes rather than consuming them. Those who have families are supporting them, rather than letting them become another burden on welfare rolls (Goss, 1989). In most cases, electronically monitored offenders contribute to the cost of running the program.

Recent studies of the IPS programs in California indicate that the increase of surveillance alone had little effect on recidivism. The combination of supervision with employment, counseling, and other correctional activities such as restitution and community service appear to be effective (Petersilia & Turner, 1990).

Another important theoretical underpinning of EM is that of just deserts, making the punishment fit the crime. With relatively few sanctions between incarceration and regular probation, EM decreases the punitiveness of conventional incarceration by allowing offenders to stay at home, and yet increases the strictness of supervision by constantly monitoring offenders' movement during curfew hours. In this sense, the decision concerning offenders' sentences is based, not upon their needs, but upon the penalties that they deserve for their acts. Punishments are graded on the seriousness of the crime for which the offender stands convicted and the seriousness of his/her prior record (Von Hirsch, 1976).

Without intermediate sanctions, offenders with less serious crimes pose a dilemma for the court. Their prior record and current convicted offense do not warrant incarceration, but regular probation cannot provide the punishment deemed appropriate for the offender. For those who are caught between the two traditional sentences, EM fills an important role of ensuring that justice is carried out.

ELECTRONIC MONITORING IN LOS ANGELES COUNTY

In search of innovative intermediate sanctions, the Los Angeles County Probation Department has initiated a series of programs in recent years to provide judges with more alternatives. These programs include intensive supervision, narcotic testing, work furlough, restitution, and home detention with electronic monitoring.

EM in Los Angeles County was initially experimented with as an enhancement to probation supervision, such as the IPS for high-risk probationers. Later it was introduced to alleviate local jail crowding, such as pretrial release and work furlough. In both cases, EM was applied to high-risk offenders who would normally wind up in jail cells. The use of EM for these high-end offenders rather than drunk drivers or other misdemeanants were mostly out of concern for pubic safety and community protection. As more and more serious and chronic offenders are placed on community corrections, the assurance of community safety and prompt revocation of recidivated offenders became the highest priority for the Probation Department.

However, EM has mostly been tried on a small scale with little impact on the overall population. The diminishing resources at the local level have limited the development of electronic monitoring programs in the county. The sheer number of probationers in the county also makes it hard to implement any EM program on a meaningful scale. However, EM has been piloted by several state and federal grant-funded programs. The experience in general has been positive while the results are somewhat mixed. With these trial programs, the Probation Department has gained tremendous understanding of the nature and efficacy, as well as the limitations, of electronic monitoring.

The following is a brief description of these programs and how electronic monitoring has been used in different contexts. For more detailed information regarding each program, readers may contact our department.

The Electronic Surveillance Program (ESP)

This was the Probation Department's first pilot project to use electronic monitoring equipment to enhance intensive probation supervision. This program was funded through a federal grant from the Bureau of Justice Assistance. At the time of its implementation in 1986, it was the only electronic surveillance program in the nation targeting high-risk offenders. This program was operated in the context of intensive probation supervision, as a comparison to increased human surveillance.

Offenders were screened for eligibility by using the Wisconsin Risk Assessment Scale, an objective scoring system that categorizes offenders based on factors such as crime type, prior record, employment history, and drug use. More than one-half of the participants were convicted of drug offenses and 15 percent were violent offenders. They all had extensive prior records, averaging six to seven prior arrests, one prior felony conviction and two to three misdemeanor convictions.

The goal of ESP was to reduce recidivism through close supervision, quick revocation of violators, and programs of rehabilitation. The central theme was close surveillance and tough response to violators. Participants were placed on active (continuously signaling) electronic monitoring for a period of 90 days. Following that they were placed on home restriction without electronic monitoring but with more frequent contacts with probation officers who handled smaller caseloads—an average of 33 per officer. After a year, they proceeded to routine probation with caseloads of about 250 per officer. A total of 49 probationers participated in the pilot project.

The evaluation found that although the supervision was intensive and response was prompt, EM actually increased the likelihood of condition violation and had no significant effect on re-arrests as compared to the regular probation group (Petersilia & Turner, 1990). This appears to be an inevitable consequence of close supervision, which makes it much easier to detect any noncomplying behavior. Although the findings were discouraging with respect to the original goals, they raised many issues with regard to how supervision outcomes should be measured. From the objectives of control and public safety, a high recidivism rate and quick removal of violators should be seen as a success. But from the perspective of rehabilitation, a high recidivism rate means failure.

Apparently the future of electronic monitoring depends on how one justifies what EM is supposed to accomplish. Petersilia and Turner (1990:99) suggested the most compelling reason for continued development of such intensive supervision is the objective of just desert. The long-standing need for intermediate sanctions justifies the continued use of intensive supervision with electronic monitoring, which is less punitive than incarceration but more so than regular probation.

The Supervised Release Program

This program was originated from the county's Superior Courts. It offers a release mechanism to reduce jail crowding by releasing defendants, charged with a felony, to electronic monitoring supervision. These offenders do not qualify for release on their own recognizance.

Participants are assessed on their past criminal history, the seriousness of the immediate offense and the degree of community ties that would maximize the likelihood of his/her appearance for all scheduled court dates. The program only takes those deemed to be "good risk." Some of the defendants are also required to participate in a program of drug testing or treatment during this period.

In the initial implementation stage, the Supervised Release Program supervised 63 defendants from the time of its implementation in April 1990 through October 1991. Defendants participated in the program an average of 71 days. One defendant was arrested while participating in the program. The program reported having saved 2,786 jail days, translating to a savings for the county of $768,519. Currently the program supervises 50 defendants. This is an in-house supervision program primarily designed to relieve jail overcrowding, and no systematic evaluation has been carried out to examine the value of EM in this context as opposed to other types of pretrial release.

The Work Furlough Electronic Home Detention Program

This is another effort by Los Angeles County to alleviate jail crowding, except that the program targets those already sentenced to jail. Participants in the program are all county jail inmates (so far all males) who work during the day and go home on electronic monitoring at night. Normally work furlough participants have to stay at the county-run facilities for off-work hours. This program is unique because participants help pay for the administration of the supervision program and at the same time avoid using the county jail facilities. Inability to pay does not preclude participation in the program. However, any participant can be sent back to jail at any time if it is determined that he has failed to comply with the conditions of his home detention.

Since its inception in May of 1989, 416 inmates have participated in the program. The total cost avoided through January 31, 1993 is $1,097,545 (figured at $40 per day county jail cost). During this period, the county has also collected another $486,254 from the program. This is an in-house service intended to monitor inmates after work hours and reduce county jail cost and no systematic evaluation has been carried out.

Community Detention Program (CDP)

This is the only EM program targeting the juvenile probation population in the county. It is designed to relieve juvenile hall crowding. This is a non-secure detention program that serves to restrict a minor's movement in the community pending court disposition. Various levels of supervision and surveillance are instituted based on the determined level of threat to the minor, other persons, or property. All minors referred to the CDP have restrictive conditions placed upon them similar to detention in juvenile hall; however, not all of them are subject to electronic monitoring surveillance.

Since the beginning of the program in June 1990, a total of 973 juveniles have participated in the electronic monitoring component. They spent an average of 37 days under electronic surveillance. An internal evaluation reported that 11.5 percent juveniles violated their conditions of probation and another 4.5 percent were re-arrested during the program. The majority, 87 percent, successfully completed the program.

Since the program was set up primarily to alleviate juvenile hall crowding, the saving was rather impressive. By the end of 1992, the Department avoided a total of $2.8 million by reducing juvenile hall days (figured at $78 per day juvenile hall cost). No studies have been done to evaluate this program as compared to its nonelectronic surveillance cases.

The Gang Drug Pushers Program

This program was developed in response to the growing involvement by identified adult gang members in drug-related violence. Same as the ESP, this program was surveillance-oriented. It was thought that the implementation of electronic monitoring targeting adult gang pushers would provide effective and closer supervision—quick identification and revocation of those who are involved in drug-related activities, and expedite their removal from the community when warranted.

This pilot program was funded by the California State Office of Criminal Justice Planning and was operated by two deputy probation officers, each with caseloads of approximately 25 probationers. The goal was to provide maximum community protection through intensive supervision. The targeted population for the program was classified as high risk, adult gang members who had been convicted of a drug-related offense.

The program began in February 1987 and supervised 158 probationers during its five-year period. Most of the participants in this program had been incarcerated first, then released to the electronic monitoring program for an average of 60 days. The internal administrative statistics revealed that 85 percent of the probationers were either arrested or found in violation of probation conditions prior to the program completion; 40 percent of the probationers were remanded to state prison. This project appeared to support the finding that EM significantly increases supervision intensity and enables prompt response to noncomplying behavior, thus protecting the community; but at the same time, it also induces a high level of recidivism.

Narcotic Electronic Surveillance Program (NESP)

This was a joint venture between the Los Angeles County Probation Department and the University of Southern California, and funded by the National Institute of Justice. The project was intended to provide judges and decision-making officials with knowledge about the validity and cost effectiveness of electronic monitoring for drug offenders with an order for narcotic testing as a condition of probation. These offenders make up the majority of inmates currently housed in our county jail facilities.

To address the jail overcrowding problem, intensive probation supervision with electronic monitoring has been considered as an alternative to long-term incarceration in the county jail. But the lack of funding has so far kept it from being tried out on a larger scale.

Despite some difficulties in carrying out the project, NESP has remained the most comprehensive and rigorously controlled effort to evaluate EM in Los Angeles County. It was carried out in two quasi-experiments, plus two components of controlled experiment, one comparing active with passive monitoring equipment, and one assessing the contribution of an added night-response officer in supervision of the monitored probationers. The two quasi-experiments compared 126 electronically monitored probationers with 200 regular probationers. Researchers conducted in-depth interviews with more than one-half of the electronically monitored offenders to examine how the monitoring affected their life and daily activities.

The findings had many positive implications for continued use of electronic monitoring for this type of offender (Glaser & Watts, 1992a). For those who were employed at the time their probation began, there was not much difference for the experimental group and comparison group; but for those unemployed or "poor" in financial status, electronic monitoring proved to be significantly more effective than regular probation. Electronically monitored probationers had significantly fewer arrests and condition violations. There was also a significant increase in conventional activities, such as tending house chores, early to bed and early to rise and interactions with their families. These positive changes diminished after the monitoring, but did not disappear. The evaluation also found that there were no significant differences in outcomes between the two types of electronic monitoring devices, active (continuous monitoring with radio transmitter) and passive (intermittent checking through programmed telephone calls).

An important implication of the findings is the identification of the group of probationers for whom EM may work well. For these offenders, house arrest with electronic monitoring appeared to have both deterrence and rehabilitative value. Despite the significant increase of resources in staffing and monitoring cost to supporting such a program, electronic monitoring has proved to be less expensive than incarceration and more effective than either jail or regular probation in reducing recidivism (Glaser & Watts, 1992b).

The Electronic Monitoring/Home Detention Program (EMs)

This is the County's most recent program and was developed as a model of public/private partnership in response to a growing concern over the lack of established standards in EM and private companies' inability to access criminal backgrounds of those being monitored. It was a result of an evaluation of all EM programs (public and private) operating in the County by the Probation Department in conjunction with representatives from all local judicial districts.

EMs were designed primarily to carry out home detention orders for non-probation cases. Three privately contracted companies provide electronic monitoring and related home detention services under the direction and oversight of the Probation Department. The entire program is funded by fees paid by the offenders. This is also the program that spearheads the innovative "equality fund" whereby a percentage of the private companies' gross revenue is used to subsidize indigent offenders.

Participants are screened by the Probation Department prior to their enrollment in the program and the private companies follow specific guidelines in monitoring their activities. Offenders with a history of or conviction for violence or sex crimes are excluded from program participation. Also excluded are offenders with convictions of drug sales or manufacture. In cases where the offender is on formal probation, enrollment and completion notices and any violations are reported to the supervising probation officer. In other cases, the information is reported directly to the court.

Since its inception in October 1992, 338 offenders have participated in the program. A majority of them are first-time offenders. Statistics are being maintained for future analysis to determine success in the areas of rehabilitation and recidivism and, among other things, which types of offenders involved in which types of offenses are most likely to perform well on EM.

The Probation Department closely monitors the performance of the service providers by conducting frequent, unannounced audits of offender case files and monitoring reports. As the "fine-tuning" process continues, we will be able to establish countywide and, possibly, statewide standards in this relatively new industry at no cost to the taxpayer.

EQUIPMENT SELECTION AND CRITERIA ESTABLISHMENT

In Los Angeles County, both active (continuous monitoring) and passive (programmed contact) have been used. Continuous monitoring (radio frequency) equipment will notify monitoring personnel whenever the offender enters or leaves his/her residence. A small transmitter is attached to the offender with a security band that cannot be removed without generating a tamper alarm. A receiver is connected to the offender's home telephone line and continuously receives the transmitter's signal as long as the transmitter is in range, usually 150 feet in radius. This receiver also picks up a tamper alarm if the security band is broken or cut and automatically reports all activity to the monitoring center every few minutes via normal phone lines.

The passive monitoring device places telephone calls according to a pre-programmed schedule to the offenders' residence during their hours of home detention. These phone calls are computer-generated at random with the number of calls determined by the monitoring agency. The offender answers the phone and verifies his presence in the residence electronically by placing a small wristlet into a verification unit attached to his/her phone line. This wristlet is attached with a security band similar to the bands used by the continuous monitoring systems.

In the past, the passive system required voice verification where the offender repeats key phrases that have been previously recorded and reduced to a digital voiceprint. When the voiceprints match, verification of the offender's presence at his/her residence is completed. Both programmed contact systems are capable of recognizing recorded voice (answering machines) and call forwarding, and will not complete verification under these conditions. With the advance of technology, voice verification has been replaced by video image. The offender now must look into the micro camera that captures his/her image and relays it back to the monitoring office where it will be verified by the staff with his/her picture on file. This improvement has simplified the verification process and significantly increased the reliability of the monitoring process.

Problems with both kinds of equipment were reported in the past. For instance, the passive equipment did not work on all telephones. Some special services, such as call waiting, had to be canceled. The signal from the active equipment could be grounded by a large metal cabinet, metal lath in a wall, or other conductors, especially if they were connected to water pipes. These problems have become rare with the advances in technology.

But most recent complaints are related to some special circumstances where the monitoring device can be an awkward inconvenience in life. The randomized calls may occur early in the morning, repeatedly awakening the offender's entire family. Many offenders feared that playing their TV or running their vacuum cleaner would drown out the telephone's ring. With improvement in technology and the use of both systems simultaneously on the offender, most of these problems and complaints have been corrected.

The cost of the continuous monitoring systems has an average cost of six dollars per day; and the passive system costs three dollars per day. The two systems can be used separately or simultaneously depending upon the offenders' perceived risk to violate. Currently most vendors choose to use both.

The selection of vendors to provide monitoring services has been an experience of great significance for the Probation Department. The private sector components and the government agency must learn to work with each other and adapt to each other's style. The checks and balances among the milieu of needs for profit and efficiency, accountability, and legal oversight oftentimes become a delicate work of art that requires understanding, patience, and even tolerance.

Although private companies have been providing electronic monitoring services in Los Angeles County for several years, there were no set standards of operation. Because participants paid a fee to the company, it was sometimes in the company's best interest not to report a violation for fear of losing a client. In some cases, fly-by-night monitoring companies would not report curfew violations as long as the client paid his or her bill. When found out, they would simply go out of business and open in another area of the county under a different name.

In some programs, the Probation Department was responsible for screening and recommending potential candidates to the court for monitoring, and supervising the entire operation. In other instances, some private vendors had direct access to judges who would order non-probation cases directly for them to monitor. However, when the Probation Department was not involved in supervision, private companies had no access to criminal histories. As a result, no proper screening and investigation were done for these cases; an individual with an extensive criminal history may appear before the court on a low-level misdemeanor offense and be allowed to participate in home detention based solely on the circumstances of the instant matter. In one such case, a participant in an EM program left his home and committed murder.

Due to the lack of coordination in these EM programs and a growing concern about home detention programs, the Los Angeles Board of Supervisors recently instructed the Probation Department, in conjunction with other members of the county justice system, to evaluate and recommend the best way to carry out this new form of criminal justice sanction. This joint evaluation effort concluded that a public-private partnership could best address these concerns, whereby private companies would provide the actual monitoring services while the Probation Department would maintain oversight and administrative responsibilities. As a result, all future EM activities in Los Angeles County will have to be initiated and coordinated by the Probation Department.

In its latest development of the Home Detention Program, the Probation Department sent out a Request for Proposals (RFP) to solicit qualified contractors. The RFP included a performance work statement. All interested contractors attended a bidder's conference. The evaluation process consisted of two phases. The first phase included an evaluation of the cost to the offender, the percentage of contractor profit offered for administrative services, and the soundness of the proposed monitoring services. At the end of this phase, all proposals received a composite score and were ranked from high to low. In the second phase, the top six rated contractors were invited to make a verbal presentation to the evaluation committee. As a principle, the committee selected three vendors to maintain competition and prevent monopoly. The final decision to select the three vendors was made by the chief probation officer.

GETTING THROUGH BUREAUCRATIC BARRIERS

Getting a new program started always means a long list of bureaucratic hurdles to overcome. The implementation of EM means the acceptance of new concepts, new supervision tools, new people to work with, and new ways of conducting otherwise routine activities. These changes and adjustments oftentimes mean more work and inevitably invoke resistance from highly autonomous officials, from judges and prosecutors to probation officers and their union.

As in the example of NESP, although endorsed by the Chief Probation Officer, the program could not be carried out as originally planned. The total number of cases referred to the program was far below the predicted figure. In fact, for the initial three to four months, only two cases were ordered by the court to the EM program. Through personal contacts and interviews, the researchers became aware that probation officers were reluctant to refer cases to the program because it would entail extra work for which they had no time (Glaser & Watts, 1992a:12). Later, the union stated that any major increase in the probation officer's workload required union approval in advance.

An influential judge was widely reported to have said at a meeting of judges that the experimental design of the program (randomized case assignment) would destroy the credibility of the court's sentencing and should not be tolerated. In fact, the actual sentencing of offenders to the program became rather arbitrary with terms varying from 60 days to 120 days. Although the original proposal clearly stated 45 days of monitoring for the purpose of evaluation, the judges imposing the sentences were not constrained by program guidelines. Those sentenced to EM were mostly probation violators rather than the requested original sentences.

In short, the experimental design had to be changed to a quasi-experimental study, severely limiting the validity of the evaluation and the power of inference. This program demonstrated that controlled experimentation is often not feasible, even when it is authorized and assured because of the realities of the justice system.

These bureaucratic barriers and resistance persist as long as changes are required, even if the program is initiated from within the government. As in the example of the Home Detention Program, it was our original intention to start the program in three target court jurisdictions in the county and then branch out to other courts once the program was operating smoothly. However, one vendor had already been operating an electronic monitoring service in Los Angeles County for several years. The court continued to sentence offenders to the vendor as established by their prior contracts. The Probation Department therefore has become a "sales" person to promote the new program and the referral criteria and procedures to judges and clerical staff in 34 Municipal and 11 Superior Courts in Los Angeles County. For those judges who were against electronic monitoring as an alternative sanction due to prior bad experiences with faulty equipment or unscrupulous companies, the Probation Department had to meet with them and explain the extensive research and development processes and demonstrate the effectiveness of the equipment.

Although the response from most meetings was positive and judges and district attorneys have become more receptive to the idea of EM as an appropriate sanction, the efforts and responsibilities of the Probation Department as the leading agency and coordinator in this new EM program were tremendous.

THE INDIGENT FUND AND EXTENDED SERVICES

In Los Angeles County, all EM programs are either saving money for the county, as in the case of pretrial release, or self-sustaining. In most cases, participants pay for the monitoring service and administrative fees. The financial independence has enabled these programs to survive the worse fiscal budget crises facing the county in recent history.

The average cost of an EM program is currently $15 per day; however, all vendors utilize a sliding scale and charge is based on the offender's ability to pay. To provide electronic monitoring service to offenders of all income levels, a unique funding mechanism was created whereby the private companies give 20 percent of their gross revenue to subsidize indigent offenders and cover the cost of probation staff involved in oversight and monitoring of the program. This arrangement enables government to establish standards in a new industry at no cost to taxpayers.

In all previous (some still existing) EM programs involving probationers, vendors were required to provide only equipment and monitoring, leaving most administrative work to the probation officers who are already overloaded with regular duties. In a recent development, the Probation Department's Electronic Monitoring/Home Detention Program contractually requires the private companies to extend their services on non-probation cases where EM is used as a substitute for jail time.

In addition to their regular monitoring, these vendors now also complete receiving procedures from the court and notify the appropriate authority of client enrollment, provide literature and referral materials (counseling centers, employment programs, etc.) to meet client needs, testify before court regarding monitoring systems if needed in any judicial proceeding, and provide other services deemed necessary to the operation of the program. These vendors may also provide court-ordered breath-alcohol testing via in-home monitoring units. It is clear that these arrangements require the private sector to carry more responsibilities than just logging activities and reporting alarms.

DISCUSSION

In Los Angeles, EM has been used in several contexts mostly because opportunities arose due to available funding and the need to explore alternative sanctions and improve probation supervision. Well-intended policymakers are interested in finding out if the tool aids in their dealing with the mounting pressure from the public to handle criminals more effectively and protect the community without much demand on the local government budget. Most of our programs have been a trial-and-error process from which we have gained tremendous first-hand knowledge of the potential value of control and rehabilitation in electronic monitoring.

In the context of jail crowding, EM has become an optimum solution because conventional probation cannot afford around-the-clock surveillance. Whether electronic monitoring has any deterrent or rehabilitative value in this context is secondary to the primary goal of watching these offenders constantly once they are placed in the community, such as in the cases of pretrial release and work furlough. Electronic monitoring here serves merely as a security camera, facilitating a quick detection of and response to any violations by the offender.

While the need for the surveillance of inmates released on house arrest is obvious, the role of EM in probation supervision is ambiguous. The measure of outcome still remains a primary source of debate. Although we are fully aware of its surveillance value, we are uncertain about its rehabilitative potential. In the RAND study (Petersilia & Turner, 1990), EM was found to have no appreciable effect on recidivism. Quite the opposite, it tended to increase the likelihood of violation detection and re-arrest. The increase of recidivism has been generally attributed to the closer surveillance and rigorous follow-up of condition violations. Intensive probation supervision with EM protects the community safety but worsens the jail overcrowding problem. This finding has taught us that without a comprehensive approach to prevent offenders from engaging in future criminal conducts, any jail overcrowding relief experienced can only be short lived. But to insure community safety and rehabilitate offenders first of all requires a significant downsizing of officer caseload size, which is intolerable to current budget allocations.

The USC study contended, however, that EM could be beneficial for unemployed drug offenders (Glaser & Watts, 1992b). Incarceration and revocation due to conditional violations are not necessary. Combined with other treatment ingredients, such as drug testing and employment training, EM can be a useful tool in rehabilitation. The question now is how to identify the population for which electronic monitoring is most beneficial. In this case, electronic monitoring is not primarily intended for deterrence and control, rather for positive changes in offenders' lifestyles and habits that impair their employability. However, this brings up yet another dilemma. Most intensive supervision cases carry court-ordered rehabilitative plans that far exceed the capabilities of services provided by local governments.

Unlike many programs across the country that handled mostly petty offenders, early electronic monitoring programs in Los Angeles focused on high-risk, even violent, offenders, in most cases as an adjunct to a probation order. The main purpose was to ensure community protection and quickly remove offenders who pose a threat to public safety. A recent development in Los Angeles County has been toward using electronic monitoring for misdemeanants and petty offenders, those who would otherwise be placed on summary probation. Technically, these offenders may receive any sentences from a fine to six months in jail. However, given the current jail crowding crises, chances of them going to jail are almost nonexistent.

These offenders have little other criminality and fair-to-good job records. They can be most cost-effectively deterred by fines, other monetary penalties and community service (Glaser & Gordon, 1990). However, the use of EM adds a more punitive aspect to their sanction which goes hand in hand with current hard-nosed policy. It serves as an extra deterrent to further criminal activity. In addition, home detention substitutes for the incarceration requirement of the sentence. Hopefully, future studies can clarify the benefits of applying EM to petty offenders as opposed to other sanctions.

Perhaps the biggest challenge for continued use of electronic monitoring is its justification. EM has been applied rather indiscriminately to perpetrators of a wide range of criminal offenses (Renzema, 1989; Maxfield & Baumer, 1990; Byrne, 1990). Early programs were generally used as an alternative to incarceration (Friel et al., 1987). More recently EM has been extended to the direct release of offenders from jail or prison to alleviate crowding, and to the supervision of unconvicted individuals held in lieu of bail. There has also been a significant shift from probation populations to parolees and unconvicted or unsentenced individuals (Renzema, 1989). The current wave of home detention has included a large number of non-prison-bound offenders who neither deserve the punishment nor need the close control (Nellis, 1991).

What is lacking is a careful assessment of the level of punishment delivered by EM. When using EM on petty offenders not on probation and with little prior criminal history, we may in fact deliver intermediate punishment to offenders who pose less risk for the community than those on traditional probation supervision. On the other hand, the high recidivism rate as a result of close surveillance inadvertently inflates the number of low-risk offenders that compete with high-risk offenders for the much-needed jail space. Until decisionmakers clarify their purpose, EM programs will continue to divert some offenders from prison, while simultaneously widening the net of social control over others.

Perhaps our concerns over the theoretical issues of using EM should be left to academic researchers. As far as the practitioners are concerned, EM appears to have multiple applications in community corrections. The intent and purpose of EM is unique to each program. For high-risk probationers, EM is used to enhance public safety and quickly identify and remove repeat offenders. For low-risk offenders, EM fills a very wide gap between incarceration and probation. It can be an effective sanction for offenders who break the law and warrant a penalty, but are otherwise productive members of society. EM in these cases satisfies the mandatory minimum jail time requirement for such crimes as multiple drunk driving and driving with a suspended license. EM, when used in conjunction with drug/alcohol testing and a treatment program, allows the offender to remain at home and adds a structure to the offender's life which he/she may never have experienced.

Wearing a device with a tangible feeling of the deterrent effect of a sanction represents a new perspective unprecedented in traditional probation supervision. The reaction of the public and law enforcement agencies to our electronic monitoring programs has been positive. Based on the past seven years of experimenting with this new form of supervision, we offer the following key points that we consider crucial if an EM program is to be implemented successfully:

1. The prior planning of an EM program must include all affected personnel and agencies from the court to probation agency, from line staff to management. The level of participation from involved personnel directly affects the operation and outcome of the program. Continuous cooperation and strong commitment from the leadership of each agency is imperative. Any resistance from any agency at any level of the bureaucratic structure can cause serious ripple effects.

2. Goals must be specific and attainable, with quantifiable measurement that allows evaluation. Systematic data collection should be established from the beginning to gather statistics on program progress and outcomes.

3. Affected offender populations must be clearly defined and studied to determine if there will be sufficient numbers of participants to justify the size of the program and produce a measurable impact on the population.

4. If the actual monitoring is done by private vendors, direct contact should be established between the monitoring staff and the supervising deputy officers. A clear articulation of responsibilities for both sides is imperative.

Electronic monitoring is still in its infancy; much more needs to be learned and studied. We are still experimenting with this newly devised punishment or surveillance tool. If jail overcrowding persists and offenders are to spend part or all of their sentences outside prison walls, electronic monitoring can be expected to play an expanded role in the criminal justice system.

2

The Juvenile Electronic Monitoring Program in Lake County, Indiana: An Evaluation*

Sudipto Roy
Indiana State University

Michael P. Brown
Ball State University

INTRODUCTION

Electronically monitored home detention has become a common disposition throughout the United States. Court-ordered home detention, and the use of electronic devices to monitor offender compliance with those court-orders, has radiated prodigiously over the last nine years. Technological advancement has made possible the use of electronic monitors for home detention. Electronic monitoring programs were first established for use with adult offenders in 1984. Applications for juveniles occurred in 1986.

Today, electronically monitored home detention for juveniles is developing at a rapid pace; however, research on the impact of these programs on offenders is limited. The growth of these programs calls for further research. Most importantly, research needs to incorporate experimental design to evaluate these programs (McShane & Krause, 1993; Rogers & Jolin, 1989).

The purpose of this study is to evaluate the impact of the electronically monitored home detention program for juvenile offenders in Lake County, Indiana. This program was initiated in February, 1990. An experimental

*Paper presented at the annual meetings of the Academy of Criminal Justice Sciences, March 16-20, 1993, in Kansas City, Missouri.

21

design is utilized to concentrate on the impact of the program on the participating offenders. Two types of home detention are used with juveniles in
Lake County—electronic monitoring and "in-house" or manual. In this study,
electronic monitoring is used as an experimental group and in-house/manual
is used as a comparison group. The impact of the program is measured in
terms of offender compliance with home detention requirements and offender
recidivism subsequent to their successful exit from home detention.

RESEARCH ON JUVENILE ELECTRONIC MONITORING PROGRAMS

Empirical studies focusing on the impact of electronic monitoring programs on juvenile offenders have been reported since the late 1980s. Most of
the information available on these programs contains only reports on the number of juveniles successfully completing their programs. Only a few studies
concentrate on the impact of these programs on lowering offender recidivism.

The Forsyth County Office of North Carolina Division of Youth Services
is the first jurisdiction known to have used electronic monitoring for juveniles. The program is used in an aftercare setting. However, participation in
the program is voluntary. Clarkson and Weakland (1991:4) report that this
community detention program "became successful in assisting juvenile
offenders with returning home from detention." According to their report, 11
youths (out of a total of 16 youths) successfully completed the program resulting in a 68 percent success rate. The report does not include any follow-up
study on offender recidivism after their exit from the program.

Another aftercare electronic monitoring program for juveniles administered in Kenosha County, Wisconsin, reported that 70 percent of the juveniles
completed a pilot project in 1987 and 53 percent completed a second pilot
project in 1988 (Editor, *Journal of Offender Monitoring*, 1990). Ten juveniles
participated in the 1987 pilot project. During the second pilot project in 1988,
19 juveniles were placed on electronic monitoring.

Vaughn (1991) conducted a survey of nine juvenile programs in 1988.
According to this survey, the percentages of successful completion ranged
from 70 percent to 95 percent. For instance, in the Orange County,
California, program (administered by the County Probation Department), 75
percent of the participants successfully completed their program. All nine programs reported in the survey included both first-time offenders as well as
repeat offenders. Also, juveniles participated in these programs at pretrial
detention and post-adjudication detention stages. Regarding offender recidivism, Vaughn (1991:199) reports—"recidivism figures are not yet available."

During the late 1980s, Charles (1989:165) studied the Allen County,
Indiana, juvenile electronic monitoring program and reported that 67 percent

of the participants successfully completed the program. In this post-adjudication program, "each of the juveniles [total of six male juveniles] accepted into the program had a history of minor criminal activity, and each had been dealt with by the court, and the Juvenile Probation Department on earlier occasions." Despite previous offense history of all the participants, offender recidivism subsequent to termination of their program is overlooked in the study. Charles (1989:152) maintains that "in terms of quantitative research design, this study must be considered exploratory in nature due to that fact that . . . there were a small number of juveniles placed on electronic monitoring [and] . . . there was no control group."

Kuplinski's (1990) survey of voluntary participation of juveniles and adults in electronic monitoring in six counties across Virginia found that 90 percent of the participants successfully completed their program requirements since 1986. However, Kuplinski does not indicate the number of juvenile participants and how many of them were successful in completing the programs. In addition, there is no follow-up study of offender recidivism (especially for adjudicated juveniles) after termination of their program supervision.

Two studies report on electronic monitoring and recidivism during the 1990s. The first, a study of offender recidivism after release, was conducted by the Office of Criminal Justice Coordination (1991) on electronic monitoring at the Orleans Parish Youth Study Center. The Center established this intensive home supervision program for pretrial youths in 1988. Overall, 127 juveniles voluntarily participated in the program. The reported rate of successful completion was 71 percent. Rearrests (16%) and technical violations (13%) were the main reasons for failure to complete the program. Also, 38 percent of the participants were rearrested subsequent to their release from the program; however, the researchers did not specify the length of follow-up to report rearrest.

The second (Editor, *Journal of Offender Monitoring,* 1990) study was conducted in Kenosha County, Wisconsin, and reported that during the 1987 pilot project, three out of 10 youths (33%) reoffended while under program supervision. Also, two juveniles (10%) out of a total of 20, recidivated during the 1988 pilot project. Electronic monitoring in Kenosha County is used as an intensive supervision component of their Aftercare Program (before juveniles are discharged from the court and after their institutionalization). Notwithstanding this situation, there was no information about offender recidivism subsequent to their release from the program.

Overall, the above discussion points to a number of facts. First, very limited research has been conducted on the impact of electronic monitoring programs on juvenile offenders. As for those that have been conducted, they mostly report the percentages of successful completion of programs. All the programs involved first-time offenders as well as repeat offenders. Yet, the available studies do not specifically indicate how many of these two groups of juveniles were successful in completing their programs. Likewise, they do not specify how many juveniles completed their programs at pretrial detention and post-adjudication detention stages. Second, it appears that "reduction in offender recidivism" has not been an issue of concern for program administrators or the evaluators. Consequently, information about offender recidivism after release from the program has been reported by only one study (Office of Criminal Justice Coordination, 1991). Information about program completion only indicates an offender's behavior over a short period of time—only during the program supervision. Recidivism data, on the other hand, can provide more information about offender behavior over broader periods of time. Recidivism is a practical outcome measure for evaluating correctional programs. As Rogers and Jolin (1989:143) point out, "recidivism is the standard by which correctional programs have traditionally been judged."

Most of all, juvenile electronic monitoring programs currently administered are not typically designed for evaluation. True experimental design needs to be incorporated in evaluating these programs (McShane & Krause, 1993). Most studies are simply reviews of cases under comparable circumstances. This makes it difficult to interpret the results—whether electronic monitoring really has an impact, or whether some aspects of supervision are liable for the seemingly high percentages of successful program completion. It is conceivable that some extralegal factors, such as the offender's family or community could contribute to an offender's positive behavior during the program supervision. The fact is, as McShane and Krause (1993) maintain, that a useful study would be one that compared groups of similar offenders under variations of supervision programs, concentrating on the impact of the programs on offender compliance with program requirements, as well as on offender recidivism.

LAKE COUNTY ELECTRONIC MONITORING PROGRAM FOR JUVENILES

The Superior Court of Lake County, Juvenile Division, established an electronic monitoring home detention program for juvenile offenders in February 1990. The Home Detention Electronic Monitoring Unit of Lake County Community Corrections administers the program and the officials (not probation officers) of this unit are responsible for monitoring the clients in the program. The Lake County electronic monitoring program was instituted for the following reasons: (1) to restrain overcrowding at the Lake County Juvenile Detention Center, and (2) to aid the Lake County Juvenile Court in meeting state mandates regarding the detention of juveniles by offering a cost-effective and noninstitutional alternative for juvenile detention.

There are several important objectives of this program: (1) to remove the stigma attached to short-term incarceration at the Lake County Juvenile Detention Center by allowing youths to remain with families; (2) to allow juvenile offenders to complete their education by allowing them to continue with school attendance, or by encouraging those who left school to return; (3) to assist juveniles in helping to support themselves and/or their families, by allowing them to continue with and/or assist them in obtaining employment; (4) to require the parents/guardians of juveniles to assume financial responsibility for supervising the child; (5) to encourage the child and parent to have a closer relationship and maintain a normal home and school environment; (6) to encourage the parent to be responsible and supportive while the court assumes the more authoritative role; (7) to maintain close supervision of juveniles by making weekly visits to their homes, schools, workplaces, etc., and by making several personal phone contacts every week, in addition to those generated by the monitoring equipment; and (8) to control the average daily population at the Lake County Juvenile Detention Center by removing children from secure detention whenever possible (Juvenile Center, 1991). Interestingly, "reduction in offender recidivism" is not included among the program objectives.

Pursuant to Indiana Code 31-6-4-5, any child who is eligible for detention at the Detention Center is eligible for home detention. Additional criteria for placement in home detention include: First, no child accused or adjudicated of a Class A felony is eligible for the program. Second, only those juveniles accused or adjudicated of a Class B misdemeanor to a Class B Felony, excluding any offense involving bodily injury or use of a deadly weapon, would be considered. In making the decision, the Juvenile Court must consider the following: (1) whether the child, if not detained, would be a danger to the community; (2) whether the child would be a danger to himself/herself; and (3) whether the child would, in all likelihood, not appear in court should he/she not be detained. Third, status offenders as well as violators of court orders can be considered for the program. The primary group of status offenders that would be considered would be runaways who can be legally detained pursuant to Indiana Code 31-6-4-5(c) for a period no longer than 24 hours, unless the detention period occurs on a weekend or a holiday. Additionally, adjudicated runaways and truants can be held for a maximum of 30 days for violations of court orders, pursuant to Indiana Code 31-6-7-16. Fourth, only juveniles who reside in Lake County and are between 12 and 17 years of age can be considered. Fifth, if the child is 16 years old and not in school, legally he/she must actively seek employment. Sixth, there must be at least one parent/guardian at home at all times. Also, the juvenile must have a telephone in the home, and the telephone must not have call waiting or call forwarding. Finally, all detention orders must include an order to maintain payments of a home detention fee ($6 per day for the duration of home detention) and any other fees, if set by the court.

Once the judge, magistrate, or referee makes the decision to order a juvenile to home detention, he/she then must decide between electronically monitored home detention and in-house (manual) detention. However, no guidelines exist to guide his/her choice of a home detention program. And, as we will see later, the consequences are significant. When a juvenile is ordered on the Electronic Monitoring program, a community corrections home detention officer contacts the juvenile and his/her parents/guardians, explains the requirements and restrictions, and installs the electronic monitoring device. The Home Detention Electronic Monitoring Unit of Lake County Community Corrections uses a passive system to monitor the juveniles in the program. The central computer at the Unit is programmed to make six daily (random) phone calls to the child's home and the child is required to appear before the camera devise connected to the home phone. Voice and visual verification methods are used to insure offender compliance. In addition, a community corrections home detention officer makes personal phone contacts two to three times a week, and visits the client at home, school, and/or workplace at least once a week, to insure the juvenile's compliance with home detention rules. The frequency of these phone contacts and visits varies according to the type of offense for which the client has been placed in the program. Also, a child ordered to the program is encouraged to participate in selected activities (e.g., medical, psychological, mental health treatment, counseling for drug/alcohol abuse) approved by the court. The average duration of home detention (about 30 days) is comparable to the average length of stay at the detention center (about 35 days). However, a juvenile can be removed from the program for violation of home detention rules (technical violation) and/or commission of a new offense. For technical violations and/or new offenses, the juvenile returns to court for further court processing. Otherwise, offenders are discharged from the court by the judge, or the magistrate, based upon their compliance with home detention requirements.

RESEARCH METHODS

This study compared an experimental group (electronic monitoring home detention group) with a comparison group (in-house/manual home detention group) matched and selected from the Lake County Superior Court Juvenile Division's home detention caseload. The primary matching variables included race, gender, age, years of education, and offense type (misdemeanor/felony) for home detention. Comparison cases were under supervision during the same time period as the experimental group. The focus of this study is the impact of electronic and manual home detention programs on offender compliance with program requirements (i.e., completion of programs) and on offender recidivism subsequent to their release from the programs.

Consequently, this study examines the following null hypotheses: (1) there is no difference in program completion between the electronic and the manual home detention groups, and (2) there is no difference in post-program recidivism between the electronic and the manual home detention groups.

Data were collected from offender files available at the Home Detention Electronic Monitoring Unit of Lake County Community Corrections from February 1990 to December 1991. Data on the manual group were gathered from the Superior Court of Lake County Juvenile Division for the same time period. Seventy-two participants were randomly selected for each group, resulting in one-half samples of all the participants in the electronic and the manual home detention programs from February 1990 to December 1991. Thereafter, the records of the Lake County Juvenile Court for all juveniles who successfully completed both the home detention programs were searched through December 1992 for information on offender recidivism after release. Reports on offender recidivism are sent to the court by all law enforcement agencies in Lake County.

The dependent variable of this investigation was "outcome" in the program and was measured in terms of two components—completion of the programs and offender recidivism after exit from the programs. For the first component, completion of programs, the data were coded as "successful" and "unsuccessful." The second component, offender recidivism, refers to rearrest records (for committing new offenses) of the participants by Lake County law enforcement agencies subsequent to their release from the programs. Rearrests were classified as felony, misdemeanor, or status offenses.

Independent variables included all the primary matching variables—race, gender, age, years of education, and offense type for home detention—as well as number of days in home detention, substance abuse, prior offense history, and prior detention.

RESULTS

Descriptive data on the juveniles in electronic monitoring and manual supervision home detention, and summary statistics are reported in Table 2.1.

As is evident from Table 2.1, the two samples in the study had a number of similarities. The majority of the participants were non-white, male offenders, between 14 to 17 years of age (average age was about 15), and had between 9 to 12 years of education (average was about 10 years). Conversely, the samples had a number of dissimilarities. For instance, 65.3 percent of the youngsters under electronic supervision were misdemeanants, while 56.9 percent of the youths under manual supervision committed felony offenses leading to their court-order to home detention. As for the duration of home detention, 73.6 percent of the juveniles spent between nine and 30 days under

Table 2.1
Variables and Summary Statistics

Variables	Electronic Group (n=72)		Manual Group (n=72)	
	No.	%	No.	%
Race				
whites	17	23.6	13	18.1
nonwhites	55	76.4	59	81.9
Gender				
males	65	90.3	66	91.7
females	7	9.7	6	8.3
Age				
11-13 years	6	8.3	6	8.3
14-17 years	66	91.7	66	91.7
Years of Education				
5-8 years	12	16.7	15	20.8
9-12 years	60	83.3	57	79.2
Offense Type for Home Detention				
Misdemeanor	47	65.3	31	43.1
Felony	25	34.7	41	56.9
Number of Days In Home Detention				
9-30 days	53	73.6	0	0
31-60 days	19	26.4	40	55.5
61-98 days	0	0	32	45.5
Substance Abuse History				
yes	13	18.1	38	52.8
not noted	59	89.9	34	47.2
Prior Offense History				
yes	12	16.7	47	65.3
no	60	83.3	25	34.7
Prior Detention				
yes	6	8.3	38	52.8
no	66	91.7	34	47.2
Completion of Program				
Successful	65	90.3	54	75.0
Unsuccessful	7	9.7	18	25.0
Recidivism After Successful Exit				
yes	11	16.9	14	25.9
no	54	83.1	40	74.1

electronic supervision (average was 26 days), and 55.5 percent of the participants spent between 31 and 60 days under manual supervision (average was 60 days). At admission, thirteen juveniles (18.1%) in the electronic monitoring group, and 38 youths (52.8%) in the manual supervision group had documented histories of substance abuse. Regarding prior offense history, 12 juveniles (16.7%) in the electronic group, and 47 juveniles (65.3%) in the manual group had previous offense records. Furthermore, six juveniles (8.3%) in the electronic group, and 38 participants (52.8%) in the manual group were previously detained in juvenile detention facilities.

In terms of the dependent variable—outcome of home detention—we find in Table 2.1 that 90.3 percent of the participants in the electronic monitoring program successfully completed their court-order, while 75 percent of the juveniles in the manual supervision program were successful. The table also shows that 16.9 percent of the electronic program participants and 25.9 percent of the manual supervision program participants recidivated within one year after successful exit from home detention.

Both the electronic monitoring and manual supervision samples in the study included first-time as well as repeat offenders. Table 2.2 reports the distribution of these offenders in completing their court-ordered home detention. We find in Table 2.2 that most of the participants in the electronic monitoring program were first-time offenders. Conversely, most of the participants in the manual supervision program were repeat offenders. As for first-time offenders in both programs, most of them (93.3% in electronic program and 92% in manual program) successfully completed home detention. However, regarding repeat offenders, their completion percentages were 75 percent in the electronic program and 66 percent in the manual program. It is evident from the table that the percentages of successful completion were higher for both first-time and repeat offender in electronic monitoring program than those on manual supervision program.

Altogether, 65 juveniles in the electronic program and 54 youths in the manual program successfully completed home detention. All these juveniles (including first-time and repeat offenders in both programs) were followed through the end of 1992 for recidivism reports. The results are presented in Table 2.3. As illustrated by the table, ten (17.8%) first-time offenders (out of a total of 56 juveniles) and one (11.1%) repeat offender (out of a total of nine youths) recidivated after successful exit from electronic monitoring program. As for the partcipants in the manual supervision program, six (26%) first-time offenders out of a total of 23 recidivated after their successful exit from the program. Also, regarding repeat offenders who successfully completed manual supervision program, eight (25.8%) juveniles reoffended during the follow-up period. During the same period of time, the remaining 23 (74.2%) repeat offenders did not recidivate. Comparing the participants in both programs, we find that both first-time and repeat offenders completing manual supervision program had higher incidences of recidivism than their counterparts in electronic monitoring program.

Table 2.2
Completion of Program by Offense History of Two Samples

| | Completion of Program | | | |
| | Successful | | Unsuccessful | |
	No.	%	No.	%
Electronic Group				
first-time offenders	56	93.3	4	6.7
repeat offenders	9	75.0	3	25.0
Manual Group				
first-time offenders	23	92.0	2	8.0
repeat offenders	31	66.0	16	34.0

The types of new offenses committed by juveniles after their successful exit from electronic monitoring and manual supervision programs are reported in Table 2.4. Eleven youths recidivated after exit from the electronic program. As indicated by the table, the distribution of types of new offenses committed by them was: 45 percent felony, 36 percent misdemeanor, and 19 percent status offenses. On the other side, 14 youths reoffended after their successful release from manual supervision program. The distribution of new offenses committed by them was 57 percent felony, 28 percent misdemeanor, and 15 percent status offenses. This table demonstrates that successful participants in the manual supervison program committed more felony offenses than their counterparts who successfully completed the electronic monitoring program.

Table 2.3
Recidivism After Successful Exit by Offense History of Two Samples

| | Recidivism After Exit | | | |
| | yes | | no | |
	No.	%	No.	%
Electronic Group				
first-time offenders	10	17.8	46	82.2
repeat offenders	1	11.1	8	88.9
Manual Group				
first time offenders	6	26.0	17	74.0
repeat offenders	8	25.8	23	74.2

Table 2.4
Types of Offenses Committed by Juveniles in Two Samples
After Exit from Home Detention

	Types of offenses					
	Felony (offenders)		Misdemeanor (offenders)		Status (offenders)	
	No.	%	No.	%	No.	%
Electronic Group	5	45	4	36	2	19
Manual Group	8	57	4	28	2	15

The first hypothesis tested in the analysis was that there was no difference in completion rates of home detention between the electronic and the manual supervision program participants. A discriminant function analysis was computed to calculate the effects of the collection of independent variables on successful completion of home detention. All nine independent variables were used in the analysis. Only five (see Table 2.5) were found to be significant predictors (at .05 level) of successful completion—number of days in home detention, offense types for assignment to home detention, substance abuse history of offenders, prior offense history of offenders, and prior detention of offenders. The computed significance of each of these five independent variables was 0.000. In other words, the significance of each of these variables was less than 0.0005 ($p < .0005$). All five significant independent variables in the discriminant analysis identified a significant difference between the two groups of participants in successfully completing their home detention.

Table 2.5
Discriminant Function Analysis: Predictors of Successful Completion

Variables	Wilk's Lambda	F	Significance
Number of days in home detention	.38546	186.5	0.000
Offense type for home detention	.93542	8.07	0.000
Substance abuse	.89581	13.61	0.000
Prior offense history	.78922	31.25	0.000
Prior detention	.80409	28.51	0.000

*These significances were computed with 1 and 117 degrees of freedom.

The F statistic and the significance of difference between the two groups of participants in terms of successful completion of home detention are presented in Table 2.6. The F value (F=185.92) was obtained from the significance test of Mahalanobis' distance between groups. As indicated by Table

2.6, the computed F value was significant at .05 level in the discriminant analysis. This significant F value demonstrates that there is a significant difference between electronic monitoring and manual supervision groups in completing court-ordered home detention. That is, the findings from the discriminant analysis did not support the first hypothesis. The null hypothesis could be rejected.

Table 2.6
F Statistic and Significant Distance Between Electronic and Manual Supervision Groups in Completing Home Detention

Electronic Supervision Group	Manual Supervision Group
185.92	0.000

Another discriminant function analysis was computed to examine the second hypothesis. The null hypothesis was that there would be no difference between the electronic and the manual supervision program participants in committing recidivist offenses during the follow-up period, after their successful exit from home detention. The findings from the discriminant analysis are reported in Table 2.7 and Table 2.8.

We find in Table 2.7 that three independent variables were found to be significant predictors of offender recidivism during the follow-up period—number of days in home detention, offense type for court-order to home detention, and prior offense history of offenders. The computed significance of each of these variables was less than 0.0005 (p<.0005). These significant independent variables identified a significant difference between the two groups of participants in terms of committing recidivist offenses during the follow-up period.

Table 2.7
Discriminant Function Analysis: Predictors of Recidivism After Exit from Home Detention

Variables	Wilk's Lambda	F	Significance
Number of days in home detention	.35010	74.25	0.000
Offense type for home detention	.86098	6.45	0.000
Prior offense history	.80606	9.62	0.000

*These significances were computed with 1 and 40 degrees of freedom.

Table 2.8 presents the F value and the significance of difference between the electronic monitoring group and the manual supervision group in committing new offenses during the follow-up period, after their successful exit from home detention. As indicated by the table, the significance of the computed F value (F=73.872) was 0.000 (p<0.0005). This significant F value demonstrates that there is a significant difference between the two groups of home detention participants in terms of offender recidivism after their release from electronic and manual supervision programs. The findings from the discriminant analysis on offender recidivism during the follow-up period did not support the second hypothesis.

Table 2.8
F Statistic and Significant Distance Between Electronic and Manual Supervision Groups (Offender Recidivism After Exit from Home Detention)

Electronic Supervision Group	Manual Supervision Group
73.872	0.000

SUMMARY AND CONCLUSIONS

The electronic monitoring home detention program for juvenile offenders in Lake County, Indiana, was initiated in February, 1990. This study compared a sample of juveniles under electronic monitoring home detention with a sample of juveniles under "In-house"/manual supervision home detention. The impact of the two programs was analyzed in terms of juveniles completing the programs, and offender recidivism after their successful exit from the programs.

Despite attempts to match the two groups (in terms of race, gender, age, and years of education), it was obvious that a number of differences existed. The experimental group (electronic monitoring) included more misdemeanants (as opposed to felony offenders) than the comparison group (manual supervision). The comparison group had more records of substance abuse and had more prior involvement with the juvenile justice system. Also, participants in this group spent a longer period of time under supervision than the experimental group. The dissimilarities between the two groups resulted in differences between them in terms of offenders successfully completing home detention, and offenders recidivating during the follow-up period, after their successful release from home detention. The experimental group had higher percentage of program completion (90.3%) than the comparison group (75%). Also, the experimental group had a lower recidivism rate (16.9%) than the comparison group (25.9%) during the follow-up period.

The findings from this study point to a number of issues. First, one of the reasons for establishing the electronic monitoring program was to restrain overcrowding at the Juvenile Detention Center. Since its inception in February of 1990, this program has helped the court in maintaining the number of detainees at the center to its capacity (80 bed spaces). In other words, the court has restrained overcrowding at the detention center. However, due to the availability of electronic monitoring in Lake County, the court is utilizing this avenue to detain more juveniles at their homes, in addition to the detainees at the detention center. That is, even though the electronic monitoring program has curbed overcrowding at the detention center, its use has widened the net for intensive supervision of juvenile detention in the county. For instance, during the study period, the court assigned 212 juveniles to the detention center; in addition, during the same time period 144 juveniles were court-ordered to the electronic monitoring program.

Second, because electronic monitoring is a more efficient form of tracking juveniles than manual home detention, noncompliance is more readily documented and the activities of participants are more closely supervised. Reducing offender recidivism after release is a reasonable program goal and should be noted as such in the program's objectives.

Third, the program's objectives emphasize parental responsibility and support toward successful completion of their children's court-ordered home detention. Also, parents are responsible for payments of the daily service charges. Given this responsibility, interviews should be conducted with both the participants and their parents (or guardians) at pre-program and post-program stages. Pre-program interviews could provide their impressions and expectations about the electronic monitoring program. Also, post-program interviews could reveal their perceptions about program operations and the impact of the program. Their notions about the program could provide some helpful feedback to the program administrators.

Finally, we turn to the issue of selecting juveniles for the two types of home detention programs. The administrators of Lake County Community Corrections have instituted the same selection guidelines for both programs. At the detention hearing, the judge or the magistrate makes the final decision on which juvenile should be court-ordered to which program. Even though the two groups were matched in terms of race, gender, age, and years of education, the data suggest that a considerable amount of discretion was used in making the final decision. Substance abuse history, prior offense records, and prior detention records of the participants of the two programs reveal that the comparison group had more high-risk juveniles than the experimental group. The data indicated that court officials selected mostly those juveniles who they believed would be successful in completing their electronic monitoring program. This selective assignment of juveniles may have influenced the high completion percentage (90.3%) for the electronic supervision group.

What might account for this selectivity? First, it may reflect the fact that at this early stage of the program, the program administrators are more concerned about a high percentage of successful completions in the program by the participants. Selective assignment, or "creaming" of participants is one way to ensure high success rate. As Rogers and Jolin (1989:150) maintain, "Administrators of electronic monitoring programs affect success rates by the selection methods they employ and in the early days of any new program administrators carefully select low-risk candidates to ensure initial success." Friel, Vaughn, and del Carmen (1987) reported the same practice in their national survey of electronic monitoring programs. Also, a high success rate at the initial stage of the program signals program effectiveness in order to secure future funding. Second, selective assignment may indicate skepticism on the part of the Judge or the Magistrate that the program can be effective in terms of participants completing the program and lowering recidivism. They may believe that their skepticism of the program will change by first knowing how lower risk juveniles perform in the program.

At this early stage of the electronic monitoring home detention program, 90.3 percentage completion makes the program look impressive. It is time to involve more high-risk offenders in this supervision and then evaluate the impact of the program on a varied range of offenders—low-risk to high-risk. Office of Criminal Justice Coordination (1991).

3

Manual and Electronic House Arrest: An Evaluation of Factors Related to Failure*

Michael P. Brown
Ball State University

Sudipto Roy
Indiana State University

INTRODUCTION

Most evaluation studies of house arrest programs have focused on individual program completion rates. Few have investigated the factors related to an offender's exit status (that is, whether or not an offender completes the program) or the differences in factors related to exit status within different types of house arrest programs.

In general, there are three levels of intensity of supervision in house arrest programs. First, manual contact programs provide the least supervision, relying upon random telephone contacts and unannounced home visits by probation officers to determine whether offenders are abiding by program conditions. Second, continuously monitoring electronic telemetry programs provide the most intensive supervision. These programs have the capacity to determine when and for how long program participants leave their residences. Third, situated somewhere between these methods of supervision are house arrest programs which utilize electronic monitors to make programmed contact with offenders.

*The authors would like to thank Maureen Scoones and Robert Hemsworth for their help with data input and computer programming.

The purpose of this study is twofold: first, to determine whether level of supervision is related to program failure in manual and continuously monitoring electronic house arrest programs; and second, to examine the factors related to failure within each program.

PREVIOUS RESEARCH

A review of the literature indicates that offender selection criteria vary across house arrest programs. Two criteria common to most programs are current offense and prior criminal history. Most programs target nonviolent offenders and those with nonviolent criminal histories (Kuplinski, 1990; Blomberg, Waldo & Burcroff, 1987; Ball, Huff & Lilly, 1988; Lilly, Ball & Wright, 1987; Vaughn, 1987). Some programs exclude offenders who have charges pending or a history of escape or absconding (Kuplinski, 1990). Individual and social characteristics are also considered when determining an offender's eligibility for house arrest. Among these are substance abuse history, employment status, supportive home or family environments and stable living arrangements (Kuplinski, 1990; Blomberg, Waldo & Burcroff, 1987). Finally, some house arrest programs only supervise offenders who have been sentenced to a specific number of days in jail (Lilly, Ball & Wright, 1987).

Despite the differences in selection criteria, evaluation studies indicate that 70 to 94 percent of offenders successfully complete house arrest programs.

- 70 percent in the Palm Beach County, Florida Sheriff's Department in-house arrest work release program (Palm Beach County, Florida Sheriff's Department, 1987)

- 75 percent in a national survey (Renzema & Skelton, 1990)

- 90 percent in an evaluation of 10 electronic house arrest programs (Vaughn, 1987)

- 90 percent across six house arrest programs in Virginia (Kuplinski, 1990)

- 91 percent in the Clackamus County, Oregon electronic house arrest program (Rogers & Jolin, 1989)

- 91.4 percent in the Kenton County, Kentucky electronic house arrest program (Lilly, Ball & Wright, 1987)

- 93.5 percent across three house arrest programs (Baumer, Maxfield & Mendelsohn, 1990, as cited in McShane & Krause, 1993:137)

- 94 percent in the Palm Beach County, Florida electronic house arrest program (Friel & Vaughn, 1986)

In the only published study that compared a house arrest program with manual supervision to one using electronic monitors to make programmed contact, Baumer, Mendelsohn and Rhine (1990) found that 81 percent of the offenders in each program successfully completed their sentences. They also discovered that the factors related to failure were unrelated to the type of house arrest program.

The relatively high completion rates reported by these studies are pointed to as evidence that house arrest programs are safe, effective alternatives to incarceration. Yet, little is known about the factors related to exit status. Vaughn (1987) contends that high completion rates can be expected in county level programs since they tend to supervise low-risk offenders. Rogers and Jolin (1989) also contend that house arrest programs are successful because they divert nonserious offenders.

However, the results of a national survey of house arrest programs indicate that the offenses committed by program participants have become increasingly serious in recent years (Renzema & Skelton, 1990). For example, at the time the first national survey of house arrest participants was conducted in 1987 major traffic offenders comprised one-third of the supervised population, but by 1989 less than 20 percent had committed such offenses (Renzema & Skelton, 1990); on the rise were personal offenses (from 6% in 1987 to 12% in 1989), drug offenses (from 13% in 1987 to 22% in 1989) and property offenses (from 18% in 1987 to 32% in 1989) (Renzema & Skelton, 1990). Moreover, contrary to those who have suggested that high success rates are attributed to the nonserious nature of the offenders being supervised, research indicates that there is little difference in exit status based on offense severity (Renzema & Skelton, 1990).

Results from the national survey also reveal that an offender's age and sentence length are predictive of exit status. Younger offenders have a higher failure rate than older offenders and the likelihood of successfully exiting a house arrest program steadily increases as the length of the sentence increases, even among offenders whose sentences exceed one year (Renzema & Skelton, 1990).

THE PRESENT STUDY

Research Questions

From this review, it is clear that researchers have paid scant attention to the factors related to exit status from house arrest programs. In the present study, our objective is to investigate the factors related to exit status in manual and electronic house arrest programs. Secondly, if we find a difference between programs, we will examine the factors related to exit status within each program.

The dependent variable, exit status, is defined as success or failure in program completion. The independent variables, the factors related to exit status, include offense seriousness, sentence length, social characteristics (social stability and ties to the community), and individual characteristics (gender, race, and age). Our research will offer an additional test of Renzema and Skelton's (1990) finding that offense seriousness is not related to exit status, but sentence length and age are.

Program Descriptions

The programs under study are operated by the Oneida County Probation Department in Utica, New York. The manual supervision program existed from December 16, 1985 through December 6, 1987. On December 7, 1987, the manual supervision program was replaced by an electronic supervision program.

For both programs, program eligibility requirements excluded offenders who: (1) have a history of violent behavior; (2) are multiple felony offenders; (3) pose a high risk to the community; (4) require in-patient drug/alcohol treatment; and (5) are serving intermittent sentences. Furthermore, to be eligible for program placement, an offender must be sentenced first to jail. The term of incarceration is then changed to an equal term of house arrest. Hence, both programs serve as an alternative to jail. Neither program charges a supervision fee to the offender.

At the time offenders begin their house arrest sentences, probation officers explain the rules of the program and the consequences of violating the conditions of the sentence. Offenders are informed that if they violate the conditions of the program at any time during the term of the sentence, they will face a term of incarceration equal to that originally imposed. Additionally, if the offender is living with another person, an attempt is made to communicate the consequences of violating the conditions of the sentence.

Informing those living with the supervised offender of the conditions of the sentence is an important issue. At any time, these individuals may request that the offender be removed from house arrest and serve his/her time in jail. The house arrest staff indicate that while those living with the supervised offender say that they understand and agree to the conditions of house arrest, it is not uncommon for them to request that the offender be removed from house arrest, citing the sentence as too intrusive on their lives. Their decision is one measure of social stability.

In the manual supervision program, compliance with the conditions of house arrest is determined by making random telephone calls and unannounced home visits. Compliance in the electronic program is measured by a system of continuously monitoring electronic software and voice verification. If an offender goes beyond the range of the continuously monitoring signal, the violation relay substation automatically reports a potential violation. All potential violations are investigated by probation officers within 24 hours.

METHODS

Data Sources and Subjects

Data were collected from New York state alternative programs case monitoring forms. The manual supervision sample consists of all persons sentenced to the program from December 16, 1985 through December 6, 1987 (N=139), the actual duration of the program. The electronic supervision sample is composed of all persons sentenced to the program from December 7, 1987 through December 31, 1990 (N=392); this program succeeded the manual supervision program and is currently operational.

The variables included in the study and the coding scheme are presented in Table 3.1. The dependent variable (Exit Status) is dichotomous, coded 1 if the offender failed the program and 0 if the offender successfully completed the program. Twenty-two percent of those in the manual supervision program and 18 percent of those in the electronic supervision program exited unsuccessfully (i.e., failed) by violating the conditions of their respective programs. Data were not available to determine whether failure was the result of a new offense or technical violation.

The independent variables, individual characteristics (i.e., gender, race, and age), social characteristics (i.e., marital status, employment status, and living arrangement), case characteristics (i.e., prior convictions and current offense) and a program characteristic (i.e., days sentenced to the programs) are also presented in Table 3.1. Age, prior convictions, and days sentenced to the programs are intervally scaled. The other independent variables are coded dichotomously.

Individual Characteristics

For both programs, males comprise about 80 percent of those supervised. Thirty-seven percent of the manual supervision program and 27 percent of the electronic supervision program are nonwhite. On average, offenders in the electronic supervision program are about one year older than those in the manual supervision program.

Social Characteristics

About 75 percent of the participants in both programs are not married. While 55 percent of those in the manual supervision program are not employed, 49 percent of those in the electronic supervision program are not employed. Finally, 14 percent of those in the manual supervision program do not reside in their own homes; 30 percent of those in the electronic supervision program live with others.

Table 3.1
Descriptive Statistics and Coding Scheme

Variable	Coding	Manual Freq.	Manual %	Electronic Freq.	Electronic %
Gender					
Male	1	109	78	319	81
Female	0	30	22	73	19
Race					
Nonwhite	1	52	37	105	27
White	0	87	63	287	73
Age					
Mean		25.9		26.7	
Range		16–57		16–62	
Marital Status					
Not Married	1	100	72	308	79
Married	0	39	28	84	21
Employment Status					
Not Employed	1	76	55	192	49
Employed	0	63	45	200	51
Living Arrangement					
Not Own Home	1	20	14	117	30
Own Home	0	119	86	275	70
Prior Convictions					
Mean		3.2		2.8	
Range		0–22		0–18	
Current Offense					
Felony	1	28	20	84	21
Misdemeanor	0	111	80	308	79
Days In Program					
Mean		93.4		86.9	
Range		7–300		7–854	
Exit Status					
Failure	1	31	22	72	18
Successful	0	108	78	320	82

Case Characteristics

Although previous research has examined how offense types (e.g., DWI offenders or petty property offenders) are related to exit status, we found that the range in offense types was too broad and the number of cases in each offense type too small to examine offenses individually. Hence, this study compares felony offenders with misdemeanants. About 20 percent of the participants in both programs are felony offenders.

In the manual supervision program, the number of prior convictions ranged from 0 to 22; the mean is 3.2. Similarly, the number of prior convictions ranged from 0 to 18 in the electronic supervision program, with a mean of 2.8 prior convictions.

Program Characteristics

On average, offenders sentenced to the manual supervision program served longer terms (93.4 days) than those sentenced to the electronic supervision program (86.9 days). However, while the sentences for the manual program ranged from 7 to 300 days, the range was 7 to 854 days for the electronic program.

Empirical Specifications

Given the dichotomous coding of the dependent variable, discriminant function analysis is used to determine whether the programs statistically differ; logistic regression is used to examine the factors related to failure within each program.

Discriminant function analysis is used to measure between-group differences. Insight to these differences can be made with the help of Wilks' lambda (Norusis, 1990). Wilks' lambda ranges from 0 to 1. As the value of lambda approaches 0, variance is attributed to between-group differences. However, as the value of lambda approaches 1, variance is attributed to differences existing within each group.

Logistic regression estimates the probability that an event will occur (Aldrich & Nelson, 1984). The probability of an event occurring (coded 1) is always made in reference to another event (coded 0). For the present study, exiting the programs unsuccessfully is coded 1, while successfully exiting the programs is coded 0. To make the main effect logistic regression coefficients understandable, they are transformed into odds ratios. As an additional measure of whether offenders are likely to fail, the main effect logistic equations are used to generate predicted probabilities. Unlike logistic regression coefficients which must be interpreted in comparison to a reference group, predicted probabilities are interpreted without making conditional statements. If a predicted probability is less than 0.50, program failure is unlikely. However, a predicted probability value greater than 0.50 indicates that program failure is likely.

Correlation coefficients were calculated to test for multicollinearity among the independent variables. The coefficients are uniformly small. Hence, all of the variables are retained for inclusion in the discriminant and logit models. See the Appendix at the end of this chapter for the correlation matrices.

FINDINGS

Between-Program Differences

The results of discriminant function analysis for the first research question, whether the factors related to failure differ when the manual and electronic supervision programs are directly compared, are shown in Table 3.2. As can be seen, the two programs were found to be significantly different (F=6.639, p<.01). Two variables served to differentiate the programs; one was the individual characteristic, race (F=6.130, p<.05), and the other was a social characteristic, employment status (F=8.207, p< .01).

An examination of the values of Wilks' lambda for race and employment status indicates that while they are smaller than those for the other variables, most of the variance is attributed to within each program. Likewise, the Wilks' lambda for the discriminant function (.883) suggests that the variance is largely found within each program.

The results of the discriminant analysis suggest that attention should turn to an examination of each program. What follows is an examination of the factors related to failure within the manual and electronic supervision programs.

Table 3.2
**Discriminant Function Analysis Comparing the Manual (n=31)
and Electronic Supervision (n=72) Programs for Failure**

Variable	Wilks' Lambda	F statistic
Gender	.982	1.820
Race	.943	6.130*
Age	.993	.674
Marital Status	.985	1.524
Employment Status	.925	8.207**
Living Arrangement	.982	1.819
Prior Convictions	.995	.505
Current Offense	.999	.446
Days in Program	.993	.683
Differences between programs:	.883	6.639**

Percent correctly classified: 74
* p<.05;   ** p<.01

Within-Program Analyses

Main Effects: The Manual Supervision Program. Table 3.3 provides the logistic regression coefficients, standard errors and odds of unsuccessfully exiting (i.e., failing) the manual supervision program. Beginning with individual characteristics, race is the only variable with a statistically significant coefficient (b=1.665, p<.01). In fact, the offender's race has the largest positive relationship to the probability of program failure. The logit coefficient indicates that nonwhite offenders are 5.3 times more likely to fail the program than white offenders. Gender and age are not statistically related to program failure. Hence, contrary to Renzema and Skelton's (1990) finding that an offender's age is related to exit status, this study found no such relationship.

Two of the three social characteristics are related to program failure. Unemployed offenders are 4.6 times more likely to fail the program than those who are employed. And those who are not married are about 3.5 times more likely to fail the program than those who are married. Employment status and marital status have the second and third largest positive coefficients, b=1.528 and b=1.248 respectively. The offender's living arrangement is not statistically related to program failure.

The number of prior convictions has a small positive coefficient (b=.139, p<.05). The coefficient indicates that as the number of prior convictions increases, so does the likelihood of program failure. Furthermore, we found that current offense is unrelated to program failure and confirm the earlier finding by Renzema and Skelton (1990).

The number of days offenders are sentenced to the program is not statistically related to program failure. This finding fails to support Renzema and Skelton's (1990) finding that sentence length is related to exit status.

Table 3.3
Logistic Regression for Variables Related
to Failure in the Manual Supervision Sample (n=31)

Variable	Logit Coefficient	SE	Odds
Gender	.930	.625	2.534
Race	1.665***	.531	5.288
Age	− .047	.039	.954
Marital Status	1.248*	.705	3.482
Employment Status	1.528***	.570	4.607
Living Arrangement	.433	.657	1.542
Prior Convictions	.139**	.072	1.150
Current Offense	.260	.703	1.297
Days in Program	.003	.004	1.003
Intercept	−4.406	1.504	

X^2 Goodness of Fit= 124.073, df=129, p=.606
Percent Correctly Classified= 81
* p<.10;   ** p<.05;   *** p<.01

Main Effects: The Electronic Supervision Program. Table 3.4 provides
the logistic regression coefficients, standard errors and odds of unsuccessfully
exiting (i.e., failing) the electronic supervision program. All of the individual
characteristics are statistically related to program failure. Race (b=1.375,
p<.001) and gender (b=1.270, p<.05) have the largest positive coefficients.
Nonwhite offenders are about 4 times more likely to fail the program than
white offenders and males are 3.6 times more likely to fail than females. Age
has a small negative coefficient (b=-.047, p<.05). This supports Renzema and
Skelton's (1990) finding that the younger the offender, the greater the likelihood of program failure.

None of the social characteristics are significantly related to program failure. Marital and employment status have small positive relationships with program failure; living arrangement has a small, negative relationship.

Both of the case characteristics have statistically significant positive coefficients. Contrary to Renzema and Skelton's (1990) finding that offense seriousness was not related to exit status, the present analysis found felony
offenders to be slightly more likely than misdemeanants (b=1.071, p<.05,
odds=.34) to exit unsuccessfully. Also, the number of prior convictions has a
small positive coefficient (b=.200, p<.001), meaning that the greater the
number of prior convictions, the greater the likelihood of program failure.

Table 3.4
Logistic Regression for Variables Related
to Failure in the Electronic Supervision Sample (n=72)

Variable	Logit Coefficient	SE	Odds
Gender	1.270**	.481	3.561
Race	1.375****	.331	3.956
Age	− .047**	.023	.951
Marital Status	.058	.383	1.059
Employment Status	.327	.302	1.387
Living Arrangement	− .245	.328	.782
Prior Convictions	.200****	.045	1.221
Current Offense	1.071**	.517	.343
Days in Program	.012****	.003	1.012
Intercept	−3.485	.932	

X^2 Goodness of Fit= 382.935, df=382, p=.477
Percent Correctly Classified= 82
* p<.10;   ** p<.05;   *** p<.01;   **** p<.001

Table 3.6
Predicted Probability of Failure
in Both Programs: Social Characteristics

Variables	Manual	Electronic
Marital Status		
Not Married	.041	.031
Married	.012	.030
Employment Status		
Not Employed	.053	.041
Employed	.012	.030
Living Arrangement		
Other's Home	.018	.023
Own Home	.012	.030
Not Married + Not Employed		
+ Other's Home	.232	.034

Table 3.7 presents the probability values for the case characteristic variables. None of the probability values for either program predict failure. However, interesting differences emerge when the programs are compared.

Looking first at prior convictions, the probability values for those with no priors (minimum) and a mean number of priors are similar when the programs are compared. However, the probability of failure for those with priors matching the maximum range (22 for the manual supervision program and 18 for the electronic supervision program) is more than twice as great in the electronic supervision program (.472) than in the manual supervision program (.208). Moreover, those with a felony as the offense for which they were placed on the electronic supervision program have a probability value (.082) about 5 times larger than that for felons in the manual supervision program (.016). And the predicted probability of failure for misdemeanants in the electronic supervision program (.030) is about 2.5 times greater than in the manual supervision program (.012).

When both of the case characteristics are considered, the probability of program failure differs substantially when the programs are compared. For example, those with a mean number of prior convictions and a felony offense in the electronic supervision program (.135) have a probability of failure about 6 times greater than offenders with these characteristics in the manual supervision program (.024).

Table 3.7
Predicted Probability of Failure for Both Programs:
Case Characteristics

Variables	Manual	Electronic
Prior Convictions		
Minimum	.012	.030
Mean	.044	.051
Maximum	.208	.472
Current Offense		
Felony	.016	.082
Misdemeanor	.012	.030
Mean Priors + Felony	.024	.135

Table 3.8 provides the probability values for the number of days sentenced to the program. Probability values were calculated for selected sentence lengths, from 30 days through 730 days. The analysis indicates that none of the sentence lengths predict program failure. However, a comparison of probability values between the programs indicate divergent patterns. For example, in the manual supervision program, the probability values become larger as the sentence lengths increase. However, in the electronic supervision program, the probability values peak at 270 days and incrementally decrease through 730 days. These findings indicate that while the probability of failure increases with the sentence length in the manual supervision program, the probability of failure in the electronic supervision program increases through 270 days and then decreases thereafter.

Table 3.8
Predicted Probability of Failure for Both Programs: Days in Program

Days in Program	Manual	Electronic
30	.013	.042
60	.014	.058
90	.015	.080
120	.017	.110
180	.020	.198
270	.025	.413
365	.033	.320
547	.053	.054
730	.086	.007
Mean	.044	.051

*The authors would like to thank Maureen Scoones and Robert Hemsworth for their help with data input and computer programming.

conditions of the sentence may increase the likelihood of exiting successfully. This might be done by making employment a condition of the sentence.

For high-risk offenders, electronic monitoring appears to provide the supervision necessary to control behavior. However, for sentences extending to 270 days, it may be necessary to reaffirm the psychological and physical presence of the monitoring device. This might be done by personally meeting with the offender and reviewing his or her progress to date. At this meeting, it may be useful to show the offender a computer printout that indicates the day and time he/she was out of the monitor's range, even if permission was given to leave the residence. Also, personal telephone contacts and unannounced home visits may provide the added supervision needed to bring about conformity to the conditions of house arrest.

In conclusion, the results of this study indicate that the factors related to failure are associated with the level of supervision existing within house arrest programs. The explanations offered for the differences between the programs are subject to debate and further empirical testing.

APPENDIX

Pearson Correlation Coefficients for Independent Variables Included in the Analysis of the Manual Supervision Program

Current Status	Gender	Race	Age	Marital Status	Employ. Status	Living Arrgmnt	Prior Conv.	Offense	Days In Program
Gender	1.00								
Race	−.28	1.00							
Age	−.10	−.05	1.00						
Marital Status	.10	.12	−.20	1.00					
Employment Status	−.20	.26	.01	.01	1.00				
Living Arrangement	−.03	.02	.13	.16	.04	1.00			
Prior Convictions	.03	−.02	.34	−.25	−.14	.21	1.00		
Current Offense	.13	−.20	−.01	−.09	−.15	.05	.02	1.00	
Days In Program	.08	−.15	.06	−.01	.02	.04	.07	.36	1.00

Pearson Correlation Coefficients for Independent Variables Included in the Analysis of the Electronic Supervision Program

Current Status	Gender	Race	Age	Marital Status	Employ. Status	Living Arrgmnt	Prior Conv.	Offense	Days In Program
Gender	1.00								
Race	−.17	1.00							
Age	−.09	.03	1.00						
Marital Status	−.03	.13	−.26	1.00					
Employment Status	.08	.12	−.05	.08	1.00				
Living Arrangement	.11	.18	.04	.16	.06	1.00			
Prior Convictions	.09	−.08	.14	−.27	−.09	.06	1.00		
Current Offense	.06	−.15	.06	−.09	−.15	.11	−.16	1.00	
Days In Program	.08	−.02	.09	−.08	−.13	.02	.06	.44	1.00

Section II

BOOT CAMP

The chapters in the next section explore the increasingly popular concept of boot camps as an alternative to the use of imprisonment. Like electronic monitoring, the idea of boot camp for young offenders has a certain appeal. In a society that exhibits a high degree of concern over a perceived lack of discipline, boot camps seem to hold much promise. They generally place a strong emphasis on physical training. Boot camps aim to instill respect for authority and to build self-discipline, as have long been emphasized in basic military training. The length of time spent in boot camp programs is typically shorter than a jail or prison stay and thus can result in financial savings. And when boot camps incorporate various forms of training or treatment within the regimen, they may be able to significantly reduce recidivism rates. There has been an enthusiasm regarding boot camps as an innovative and potentially valuable alternative sanction.

In the two chapters that follow, we will see that there are many differences around the country in how boot camp programs are designed and what approaches they use to influence the behavior of offenders. There do appear to be common threads underlying most boot camp programs with respect to the assumptions about the causes of crime and delinquency. One such assumption is that law violations result in part from the disorganized and dysfunctional environments within which many offenders live. Youthful offenders in particular are often seen to be in need of some structure in their lives, and there tends to be a common belief that many young offenders do not have the basic skills or knowledge to assume a position of responsibility and productivity in society. Politicians across the political spectrum, as well as most citizens, agree that there is a "moral crisis" in the nation and that "character building" is a necessary goal in the education of young people. Boot camps have capitalized on these widespread beliefs and have begun to evolve as a major addition to the array of alternative criminal sentences.

There is reason to be both optimistic and skeptical about boot camps. It is obvious that many young men and women have greatly benefited from the training they have received in the military. There is little doubt that most young people can prosper from a better understanding of their own behavior and the self-esteem that results from participation in a challenging endeavor. There is certainly nothing wrong with attempts to instill a respect for others and to teach the value of self-discipline. To the extent that boot camps are able to accomplish these objectives, they are a welcome addition to our arsenal of criminal sanctions. Skepticism, however, has surfaced when the boot camp experience is used in isolation without attention to the other needs of offenders and with little in the way of follow-up after the release from boot camp. When used in this manner, the boot camp sanction is not likely to play a significant role in our efforts to improve the effectiveness of criminal sanctions. The two-pronged test for all intermediate sanctions has become (1) do they contribute to the alleviation of prison overcrowding? and (2) can they reduce the incidence of future criminal behavior? The future of the boot camp concept should be determined on the basis of answers to these two questions.

4

Shock Incarceration and Recidivism: An Examination of Boot Camp Programs in Four States* **

Claire Souryal
University of Maryland

Doris Layton MacKenzie
University of Maryland

"The camps instill inmates with a sense of self-respect and responsibility, which, combined with the grueling training, pushes down the recidivism rate, criminologists say." (*San Francisco Chronicle*, January 19, 1993)

"Most experts agree that without the help of family, and without addressing social problems emanating from poor

*Researchers from each state involved in the multi-site study of shock incarceration met to plan the evaluation. This was a collaborative effort. State researchers responsible for data collection included the following: Robert Kreigener and Kenneth Baugh, Jr., Florida Department of Corrections; Judy Schiff, Judith Hadley, Charlotte Beard, and Gerald Flowers, Georgia Department of Corrections; Jean S. Wall, Louisiana Department of Public Safety and Corrections; Robert McManus, South Carolina Department of Probation, Parole, and Pardon Services; Sammie Brown, South Carolina Department Corrections.

**This investigation was supported in part by Grant #90-DD-CX-0061 from the National Institute of Justice, Office of Justice Programs, U.S. Department of Justice to the University of Maryland. Points of view in this document are those of the authors and do not necessarily represent the official position of the U.S. Department of Justice. Thanks are expressed to all those who have worked on the multi-study. Requests for copies should be sent to Claire Souryal at the University of Maryland, Department of Criminal Justice and Criminology, 2220 LeFrak Hall, College Park, MD 20742.

schools, unemployment, poverty, and racial discrimination,
there is little likelihood that the 'scare' or the 'drill' will
last for any length of time." (Sechrest, 1989)

"The temptation in these troubled times, to approve of quick,
easy, even 'dirty' solutions to the problems of youth crime is
a very real one. When we are troubled, we often hurry to
'do something,' instead of being certain that what we do is
the right thing." (Hahn, n.d.)

INTRODUCTION

As illustrated above, the jury is still out on shock incarceration programs.
Regarded by some as a viable correctional option, others consider them a trendy
but ultimately unsuccessful alternative. Research released to date has not provided compelling evidence that shock incarceration programs reduce recidivism.
State departments of corrections (DOC) generally report slightly lower rates of
recidivism for shock incarceration graduates, though not significantly different
from the rates of similarly situated inmates who have served time in prison.

The balance of prior research, however, has failed to utilize statistical techniques that take into account either the time until a recidivism event occurs, or
the number of offenders actually "at risk" in the community. The present study
will attempt to address this deficiency by examining the recidivism rates of
graduates of four state-level shock incarceration programs (and comparison
samples of both prison parolees and probationers) using "survival analysis."

First, however, a general description of shock incarceration programs will
be provided, followed by a discussion of the growth of such programs nationwide, their major goals, and a review of prior research. Attention will then
turn to the study at hand with a presentation of the general methodology,
results, and conclusions.

THE SHOCK INCARCERATION CONCEPT

Shock incarceration programs (popularly known as "boot camp" prisons)
have become an increasingly common alternative sanction operating at the
county, state, and federal levels. As the name suggests, "boot camp" prisons
are modeled after the basic training of military recruits. The distinguishing
elements of these programs include: (1) military drills and ceremony; (2) physical training; (3) strict discipline; and (4) hard labor (Parent, 1989;
MacKenzie, 1990). To supplement the military-like regime, most programs
have also incorporated rehabilitative components such as academic education,
drug treatment/education, and/or counseling.

ated. The three samples of probationers included a "regular" probation sample, a sample of intensive probation supervision inmates, and a sample of diversion center graduates. Researchers also controlled for relevant demographic variables including age, race, urban v. nonurban environment, offense category, and need and risk level. After three years of community supervision controlling for demographic variables the analyses revealed the following:

Figure 4.1

Sample (N)	Returned to Prison (%)
Shock Graduate (N=860)	40.7%
Eligible Prison Sample 1 (N=768)	53.4%
Eligible Prison Sample 2 (N=840)	49.6%
Ineligible Prison Sample 1 (N=342)	55.2%
Ineligible Prison Sample 2 (N=155)	61.7%
Regular Probation Sample (N=812)	32.6%
Diversion Center Sample (N=547)	38.3%
Intensive Probation Sample (N=350)	50.2%

Adapted from Flowers, Carr & Ruback (1991:41).

Thus, shock incarceration graduates were returned to prison at lower rates than all four prison comparison groups, including those that were eligible for participation in the program.

The Illinois DOC conducted virtually the same analyses as the Florida DOC. They compared a sample of shock incarceration graduates (N=310) to a comparison sample of prison releasees who had been deemed legally eligible for the program (N=1,920) (Illinois DOC, 1992). Both groups were followed for a minimum of one year. Researchers then examined the percentage of both samples that had been returned to prison for committing either a new felony or a technical violation. The study revealed the following: (1) 5 percent of the shock incarceration graduates were returned for committing a new felony as compared with 12 percent of the comparison sample; and (2) 22 percent of the shock incarceration graduates were returned for technical violations as compared with 2 percent of the comparison sample. The DOC hypothesized that the much larger percentage of technical violations in the shock incarceration sample is due to the fact graduates are intensively supervised upon release (including 3 months of electronic monitoring), while the comparison sample is not. Thus, although shock incarceration graduates were less likely to be returned to prison for committing new crimes, they were more likely to be returned to prison as a result of a technical violation.

Similar results were found in New York (NY Department of Correctional Services and Division of Parole, 1992). Researchers compared a sample of shock graduates (N=582) to the following three comparison samples: (1) pre-shock (N=827)—offenders considered for shock but committed prior to the implementation of the program; (2) shock eligible (N=378)—offenders deemed eligible but who did not enter the program; and (3) shock removals (N=68)—offenders who were removed from the program due, for example, to disciplinary reasons and returned to prison to serve the remainder of their court-imposed prison term. Each of the comparison samples served time in prison as part of the regular prison population. The four samples were then followed in the community for 2 years. The percentages of each sample returned to prison for either new crimes or technical violations are shown below.

Figure 4.2

Sample	New Crime (%)	Technical (%)	Total (%)
Shock Graduates	17	23	40
Pre-Shock	19	25	44
Shock Eligible	20	27	47
Shock Removal	22	29	51

Adapted from the New York Department of Correctional Services & the Division of Parole (1992:124).

Again, shock graduates appear to have "outperformed" comparison samples of prison releasees, although the differences among samples are not statistically significant.

In short, based on similar analytic strategies, all four state programs (Florida, Georgia, Illinois, and New York) report comparable results. Shock incarceration graduates appear to be slightly less likely to be returned to prison than comparison samples in Florida, Georgia, and New York. In Illinois, although shock incarceration graduates were less likely to be returned to prison for the commission of a new felony, they were more likely to be returned overall due to a considerably higher rate of technical violations. Statistically significant differences among samples, however, were not reported by any state.

MacKenzie's (1991) analysis of recidivism in Louisiana can be distinguished from its predecessors due to the use of survival analysis, a statistical technique that takes into account the time until "failure" as well as the fact that the number of offenders "at-risk" in the community changes over time. In other words, estimates of recidivism are based on the actual number of offenders in the community who have not yet "failed" or exited supervision caseloads for other reasons such as legal release from supervision at the end of each month. MacKenzie also controls for the intensity of supervision and demographic variables such as age, age at first arrest, and criminal history.

Instruments. Two instruments were utilized, one to collect demographic information and the other to collect recidivism data. A "record data" instrument was used by site researchers to collect official record data. Three major categories of data were collected: (1) personal history variables such as age, race, and sex; (2) offense characteristics such as offense type and sentence length; and (3) offender criminal history such as the number of prior arrests, convictions, and most serious prior offense.

Figure 4.3

State	Samples (N)
Florida	Shock Graduates (N=112)
	Shock Dropouts (N=68)
	Prison Comparison (N=109)
Georgia	Shock Graduates (N=79)
	Prison Comparison (N=98)
	Probation Comparison (N=85)
Louisiana	"Old" Shock Graduates (N=)
	"New" Shock Graduates (N
	Shock Dropouts (N=72)
	Prison Comparison (N=
	Probation Comparison J8)
South Carolina	"Old" Shock Graduat =85)
	"New" Shock Grad (N=83)
	Prison Compariso N=64)
	Probation Comp n (N=69)
	Split-Probation mparison (N=24)

The Offender Adjustment to Community Super sion instrument was used to collect recidivism data. It is a 19-item question aire that provides information on contacts with the criminal justice s tem, including whether an offender had been arrested or jailed, had their robation or parole revoked for a new crime or a technical violation, or ad absconded. The date of the recidivism event is provided as well.

Procedure. DOC researchers complete the "record data" instrument using DOC records. The Offender Adjustment o Community Supervision instrument was mailed to supervisory agents by OC researchers. Supervising agents completed the questionnaire every th e months for a period of one year. This procedure was used in Florida and outh Carolina with the exception of the new shock sample in South Caroli a. The supervising agents of the new shock sample completed the Adjustment to Community Supervision instrument at one point in time, at the end of one year of community supervision.

In Georgia, the Adjustment to Community Supervision instrument was completed at three-month intervals by supervisory agents for a period of one year. However, due to sometimes questionable dates, researchers used the Georgia DOC computer database to validate the information collected. Reliable arrest data was not available for every subject; therefore, arrest as an outcome measure was not analyzed in Georgia.

In Louisiana, although a similar version of the Adjustment to Community Supervision instrument was used, data was collected at one point in time (between April and June, 1991). Researchers completed the instrument using records available at district probation and parole offices.

In Florida and South Carolina, samples were followed for one year of community supervision, while in Georgia and Louisiana samples were followed for two years.

Results

Sample. Samples within each state were first compared on basic demographic variables including age, age at first arrest, prior arrest(s), prior conviction(s), and offense type, to assess whether samples were reasonably equivalent at the outset of the study. In other words, did sample selection procedures, although not random, identify groups of offenders who were similar prior to the imposition of the treatment condition (shock incarceration, prison, or probation)?

Demographic Comparisons. The analyses revealed that in every state there were significant differences among samples in age at release (see Tables 4.1 through 4.3). By and large, prison parolees (split-probationers in South Carolina) were significantly older than comparison samples. While age at release and offense type were the only significant difference obtained in Florida, samples in South Carolina differed significantly on virtually every demographic variable tested. Samples in Louisiana differed significantly in both age and criminal history variables. The direction of differences in Criminal history was not consistent across states.

In short, the demographic analyses indicate that because samples differ on variables that have been found to be associated with performance on community supervision, it is essential to control for demographic variables in the analyses.

Table 4.1

Sample Demographic Comparisons from Official Records in Florida and Georgia (Significance tests refer to within state sample comparisons only.)

	Florida			Georgia		
	Shock Grads (N=112)	Shock Dropouts (N=68)	Prison (N=109)	Shock Grads (N=79)	Prison (N=98)	Probation (N=85)
Age M (sd)	19.3 (1.95)[a]***	19.0 (1.78)[a]	19.7 (1.92)[b]	20.4 (2.01)[a]***	23.4 (2.71)[b]	21.0 (2.49)[a]
Age-1st-Arrest M (sd)	—	—	—	—	—	—
Race N (%)						
Nonwhite	64 (57.1)	33 (48.5)	67 (61.5)	47 (59.5)	66 (67.4)	48 (56.5)
White	48 (42.9)	35 (51.5)	42 (38.5)	32 (40.5)	32 (32.7)	37 (43.5)
Criminal Record N (% Yes)	—	—	—	3 (39.2)***	74 (75.5)	9 (10.6)
Prior Arrests N (% Yes)	34 (30.4)	19 (27.9)	25 (22.9)	21 (26.6)***	54 (55.1)	5 (5.9)
Prior Convictions N (% Yes)	33 (29.5)	18 (26.5)	25 (22.9)	14 (17.7)***	31 (31.6)	4 (4.7)
Offense Type N (%)						
Robbery	20 (17.9)***	15 (22.1)	29 (26.6)	8 (10.1)**	13 (13.3)	3 (3.5)
Other Violent	7 (6.3)	5 (7.4)	17 (15.6)	6 (7.6)	7 (7.1)	3 (3.5)
Burglary	40 (35.7)	28 (41.2)	28 (25.7)	32 (40.5)	23 (23.5)	17 (20.0)
Theft	13 (11.6)	8 (11.8)	7 (6.4)	9 (11.4)	17 (17.4)	22 (25.9)
Drug Offenses	25 (22.3)	3 (4.4)	13 (11.9)	15 (19.0)	29 (29.6)	27 (31.8)
Other	7 (6.3)	9 (13.2)	15 (13.8)	9 (11.4)	9 (9.2)	13 (15.3)

Note: Letters not the same indicate significant differences at p<.05.
*p<.10 **p<.05 ***p<.01

Table 4.2

Sample Demographic Comparisons from Official Records in Louisiana

	Louisiana				
	Old Shock Grads (N=102)	New Shock Grads (N=117)	Shock Dropouts (N=72)	Prison (N=143)	Probation (N=108)
Age at Parole M (sd)***	23.8 (5.0)[a]	23.7 (4.7)[a]	24.5 (4.6)[a]	26.5 (5.6)[b]	24.5 (5.3)[a]
Age-1st-Arrest M (sd)	19.8 (4.1)	20.0 (3.9)	19.2 (2.9)	20.8 (5.1)	20.9 (4.6)
Race N (%)					
Nonwhite	52 (54.2)	79 (67.5)	40 (66.7)	98 (68.5)	68 (63.5)
White	44 (45.8)	38 (32.5)	20 (33.3)	45 (31.5)	39 (36.5)
Criminal History*** N (% Yes)	77 (83.7)	92 (78.6)	55 (91.7)	96 (67.6)	73 (68.9)
Prior Incarceration*** N (% Yes)	15 (16.1)	24 (20.9)	14 (23.3)	13 (9.2)	4 (3.8)
Offense Type N (%)					
Violent	7 (8.0)	18 (15.4)	6 (10.3)	18 (12.7)	8 (8.6)
Burglary	38 (43.7)	45 (38.5)	30 (51.7)	72 (50.7)	32 (34.4)
Theft	14 (16.1)	15 (12.8)	8 (13.8)	21 (14.8)	16 (17.2)
Drug Offenses	27 (31.0)	37 (31.6)	13 (22.4)	28 (19.7)	34 (36.6)
Other	1 (1.2)	2 (1.7)	1 (1.7)	3 (3.1)	3 (3.2)

Note: Letters not the same indicate significant differences at p<.05.
*p<.10 **p<.05 ***p<.01

Table 4.3
Sample Demographic Comparisons from Official Records in South Carolina

	South Carolina				
	Old Shock Grads (N=85)	New Shock Grads (N=83)	Split-Probation (N=24)	Prison (N=64)	Probation (N=69)
Age at Parole M (sd)***	20.6 (2.1)ᵃ	21.1 (2.3)ᵃ	23.4 (2.0)ᵇ	21.0 (1.9)ᵃ	21.1 (2.2)ᵃ
Age-1st-Arrest M (sd)**	18.8 (1.9)ᵃ	18.9 (2.2)ᵃ	19.4 (1.8)ᵃᵇ	18.5 (1.4)ᵃ	19.6 (2.1)ᵇ
Race N (%)					
Nonwhite**	42 (49.4)	62 (73.8)	15 (62.5)	39 (60.9)	40 (58.0)
White	43 (50.6)	22 (26.2)	9 (37.5)	25 (39.1)	29 (42.0)
Prior Arrests***					
N (% Yes)	45 (52.9)	76 (90.5)	16 (66.7)	39 (60.9)	43 (62.3)
Prior Convictions*					
N (% Yes)	32 (37.7)	41 (48.8)	14 (58.3)	38 (59.4)	29 (42.0)
Offense Type N (%)***[1]					
Other Violent	3 (3.5)	3 (3.6)	0 (—)	5 (7.8)	0 (—)
Robbery	9 (10.6)	5 (6.0)	1 (4.2)	8 (12.5)	8 (11.6)
Burglary	20 (23.5)	12 (14.5)	4 (16.7)	11 (17.2)	4 (5.8)
Theft	31 (36.5)	18 (21.7)	10 (41.7)	26 (40.6)	19 (27.5)
Drug Offenses	20 (23.5)	29 (34.9)	8 (33.3)	11 (17.2)	14 (20.3)
Other	2 (2.4)	16 (19.3)	1 (4.2)	3 (4.7)	24 (34.8)

Note: Letters not the same indicate significant differences at $p<.05$.
*$p<.10$ **$p<.05$ ***$p<.01$
[1] Note: Chi-square may not be a valid test.

Survival Analyses

The performance of offenders during community supervision was compared using survival analyses. As stated earlier, these models take into the account the time until "failure" as well as the fact that offenders may exit supervision caseloads by means other than "failure," (e.g., legal release or absconding). Two survival analysis procedures were estimated: (1) life tables (the SAS Institute Inc. [1985] Lifetest procedure); and (2) a parametric log-normal model (the SAS Institute Inc. [1985] Lifereg procedure). The parametric log-normal model was necessary in order to control for demographic variables. The four criterion variables examined included: (1) arrest; (2) any revocation; (3) revocation for a new crime; and (4) revocation for technical violation. The results of the analyses are presented fully in Tables 4.4 through 4.11. The major findings are summarized below on a state-by-state basis.

Table 4.4

Twelve-Month Life Table Survival Estimates Comparing Shock Graduate, Shock Dropout, Prison Parolee, and Probation Samples in Four States

			ARREST		
	Old Shock	New Shock	Shock Dropouts	Prison	Probation
Florida					
Month 1 (N)	112	—	68	109	—
Month 12 (N)	57	—	34	46	—
Arrested N (%)[a]	55 (49.1)	—	34 (50.0)	63 (57.8)	—
Failure Time M (sd)[1]	4.5 (3.35) (N=52)	—	5.5 (3.42) (N=29)	4.0 (2.86) (N=62)	—
12 Month Survival Est.*	0.53	—	0.56	0.43	—
Georgia					
Month 1 (N)	—	—	—	—	—
Month 24 (N)	—	—	—	—	—
Arrested N (%)	—	—	—	—	—
Failure Time M (sd)[1]	—	—	—	—	—
24 Month Survival Est.	—	—	—	—	—
Louisiana					
Month 1 (N)	102	117	72	143	108
Month 24 (N)	45	57	36	85	58
Arrested N (%)	57 (55.9)	60 (51.3)	36 (50.0)	58 (40.6)	50 (46.3)
Failure Time M (sd)[1]	9.2 (5.98) (N=57)	7.9 (4.88) (N=60)	8.1 (6.34) (N=36)	7.8 (5.99) (N=58)	8.6 (6.77) (N=50)
24 Month Survival Est.	0.45	0.44	0.48	0.54	0.54
South Carolina Split-Probation					
Month 1 (N)	85	83	24	64	69
Month 12 (N)	36	45	10	33	34
Arrested N (%)[a]	49 (57.7)	38 (45.8)	14 (58.3)	31 (48.4)	35 (50.7)
Failure Time M (sd)[1]	4.4 (3.22) (N=49)	5.6 (3.01) (N=38)	4.6 (3.10) (N=14)	4.9 (3.26) (N=31)	5.4 (3.73) (N=32)
12 Month Survival Est.	0.42	0.54	0.42	0.52	0.55

* p<.10 (Wilcoxon X^2) ** p<.05 (Wilcoxon X^2) [1] Mean time in months until "failure."
[a] Note: Arrest N (%) equals total number of arrests including cases where date of arrest is missing. If date of arrest is missing, case is censored at 1 day in survival analyses.

Table 4.5

Twelve-Month Life Table Survival Estimates Comparing Shock Graduate, Shock Dropout, Prison Parolee, and Probation Samples in Four States

			ANY REVOCATION		
	Old Shock	New Shock	Shock Dropouts	Prison	Probation
Florida					
Month 1 (N)	112	—	68	109	—
Month 12 (N)	83	—	43	67	—
Any revocation N (%)[a]	29 (25.9)	—	25 (36.8)	42 (38.5)	—
Failure Time M (sd)[1]	6.4 (2.85) (N=16)	—	6.8 (3.54) (N=11)	5.9 (2.34) (N=28)	—
12 Month Survival Est.**	0.84	—	0.83	0.71	—
Georgia (includes revocation due to abscond)					
Month 1 (N)	79	—	—	98	85
Month 24 (N)[b]	35	—	—	38	47
Any revocation N (%)	44 (55.7)	—	—	44 (44.9)	28 (32.9)
Failure Time M (sd)[1]	12.1 (6.19) (N=44)	—	—	13.6 (6.25) (N=44)	12.6 (8.15) (N=28)
24 Month Survival Est.**	0.44	—	—	0.50	0.67
Louisiana					
Month 1 (N)	102	117	72	143	108
Month 24 (N)	67	84	51	119	87
Any revocation N (%)	35 (34.3)	33 (28.2)	21 (29.2)	24 (16.8)	21 (19.4)
Failure Time M (sd)[1]	12.0 (6.11) (N=35)	10.2 (4.81) (N=33)	10.2 (6.08) (N=21)	11.2 (5.17) (N=24)	13.5 (5.61) (N=21)
24 Month Survival Est.*	0.63	0.57	0.60	0.70	0.79
South Carolina Split-Probation					
Month 1 (N)	85	84	24	64	69
Month 12 (N)	62	76	14	54	47
Any revocation N (%)[a]	23 (27.1)	8 (9.5)	10 (41.7)	10 (15.6)	22 (31.9)
Failure Time M (sd)[1]	4.7 (3.30) (N=20)	7.2 (2.56) (N=6)	6.8 (2.32) (N=6)	6.6 (1.24) (N=9)	6.3 (3.01) (N=20)
12 Month Survival Est.***	0.76	0.93	0.70	0.86	0.70

*p<.10 (Wilcoxon X^2) **p<.05 (Wilcoxon X^2) ***p<.10 (Wilcoxon X^2) [1] Mean time in months until "failure."
[a] Note: Any Revocation N (%) equals the total number of revocations including cases where date of revocation is missing. If date is missing, case is censored at 1 day in survival analyses.
[b] Note: Month 12 (N) reflects the total number at risk at Month 12 taking into account legal release in Georgia.

Table 4.6

Twelve-Month Life Table Survival Estimates Comparing Shock Graduate, Shock Dropout, Prison Parolee, and Probation Samples in Four States

	NEW CRIME REVOCATION				
	Old Shock	New Shock	Shock Dropouts	Prison	Probation
Florida					
Month 1 (N)	112	—	68	109	—
Month 12 (N)[a]	83	—	43	67	—
New Crime revocation N (%)[b]	20 (17.9)	—	12 (17.4)	28 (18.4)	—
Failure Time M (sd)[1]	6.0 (2.45) (N=10)	—	5.6 (1.52) (N=5)	5.9 (2.32) (N=20)	—
12 Month Survival Est.**	0.90	—	0.90	0.78	—
Georgia					
Month 1 (N)	79	—	—	98	85
Month 24 (N)[a]	35	—	—	38	47
New Crime revocation N (%)	33 (41.8)	—	—	38 (38.8)	12 (14.1)
Failure Time M (sd)[1]	12.0 (6.19) (N=33)	—	—	13.2 (6.11) (N=38)	15.4 (8.27) (N=12)
24 Month Survival Est.***	0.54	—	—	0.56	0.83
Louisiana					
Month 1 (N)	102	117	72	143	108
Month 24 (N)	87	106	61	126	96
New Crime revocation N (%)	15 (14.7)	11 (9.4)	11 (15.3)	17 (11.9)	12 (11.1)
Failure Time M (sd)[1]	12.6 (6.74) (N=15)	12.4 (5.77) (N=11)	9.4 (7.54) (N=9)	10.7 (4.09) (N=16)	13.2 (5.18) (N=12)
24 Month Survival Est.	0.82	0.72	0.77	0.81	0.87
South Carolina Split-Probation					
Month 1 (N)	85	84	24	64	69
Month 12 (N)[a]	62	76	14	54	47
New Crime revocation N (%)[b]	9 (10.6)	5 (6.0)	4 (16.7)	6 (9.4)	· 10 (14.5)
Failure Time M (sd)[1]	4.7 (2.96) (N=9)	7.7 (3.06) (N=3)	3.0 (—) (N=1)	6.6 (0.55) (N=5)	6.0 (2.94) (N=10)
12 Month Survival Est.	0.88	0.96	0.95	0.92	0.84

*p<.10 (Wilcoxon X^2) **p<.05 (Wilcoxon X^2) ***p<.01 (Wilcoxon X^2) [1] Mean time in months until "failure."
[a] Note: Month 12 (N) reflects the total number at risk at Month 12 taking into account technical revocations in Florida and South Carolina and technical revocations, absconding, and legal release in Georgia.
[b] Note: New Crime revocation N(%) equals the total # of revocations including cases where date of revocation is missing. If date is missing, case is censored at 1 day in survival analyses.

Table 4.7

Twelve-Month Life Table Survival Estimates Comparing Shock Graduate, Shock Dropout, Prison Parolee, and Probation Samples in Four States

	TECHNICAL REVOCATION				
	Old Shock	New Shock	Shock Dropouts	Prison	Probation
Florida					
Month 1 (N)	112	—	68	109	—
Month 12 (N)[a]	83	—	43	67	—
Technical revocation N (%)[b]	9 (8.04)	—	13 (19.1)	14 (12.8)	—
Failure Time M (sd)[1]	7.2 (3.54) (N=6)	—	7.8 (4.54) (N=6)	6.1 (2.53) (N=8)	—
12 Month Survival Est.	0.94	—	0.92	0.90	—
Georgia					
Month 1 (N)	79	—	—	98	85
Month 24 (N)[a]	35	—	—	38	47
Technical revocation N (%)	7 (8.9)	—	—	2 (2.0)	3 (3.5)
Failure Time M (sd)[1]	11.7 (7.95) (N=7)	—	—	22.5 (0.71) (N=2)	6.00 (3.46) (N=3)
24 Month Survival Est.*	0.88	—	—	0.95	0.96
Louisiana					
Month 1 (N)	102	117	72	143	108
Month 24 (N)	82	87	59	135	99
Technical revocation N (%)	20 (19.6)	30 (25.6)	13 (18.1)	8 (5.6)	9 (8.3)
Failure Time M (sd)[1]	11.5 (5.72) (N=20)	9.1 (3.98) (N=22)	10.8 (5.01) (N=12)	12.3 (7.07) (N=8)	13.9 (6.43) (N=9)
24 Month Survival Est.***	0.77	0.62	0.73	0.86	0.90
South Carolina Split-Probation					
Month 1 (N)	85	84	24	64	69
Month 12 (N)[a]	62	76	14	54	47
Technical revocation N (%)[b]	14 (16.5)	3 (3.6)	6 (25.0)	4 (6.3)	12 (17.4)
Failure Time M (sd)[1]	4.6 (3.70) (N=11)	6.7 (2.52) (N=3)	7.6 (1.52) (N=5)	6.5 (1.91) (N=4)	6.5 (3.21) (N=10)
12 Month Survival Est.**	0.86	0.96	0.74	0.93	0.83

*p<.10 (Wilcoxon X^2) **p<.05 (Wilcoxon X^2) ***p<.01 (Wilcoxon X^2) [1] Mean time in months until "failure."
[a] Note: Month 12 (N) reflects the total number at risk at Month 12 taking into account new crime revocations in Florida and South Carolina and new crime revocations, absconding, and legal release in Georgia.
[b] Note: Technical revocation N (%) equals the total # of revocations including cases where date of revocation is missing. If date is missing, case is censored at 1 day in survival analyses.

Florida

In Florida, shock graduates were compared to shock dropouts and prison releasees. The results were surprisingly consistent regardless of the outcome measure or the type of analysis (see Tables 4.4 through 4.7). The survival estimates yielded by the Lifetest procedure revealed that the shock graduate and shock dropout samples failed on each outcome measure at very similar rates. And more importantly, both shock samples (graduates and dropouts) appeared to fail at significantly lower rates than the prison sample. The Wilcoxon X^2 indicated that there were significant differences among survival curves when arrest, any revocation, and revocation for a new crime were used as the outcome measures.

When the demographic variables were controlled in the analyses, the relationships among samples held (see Table 4.8). Both shock graduates and shock dropouts were significantly less likely than the prison sample to be revoked for a new crime. When new crime revocations and technical revocations were combined, the direction of the relationship was the same for both shock samples, but only the shock graduate sample was significantly less likely to be revoked. There were no differences among samples in technical revocations. In terms of arrest, the shock dropout sample was significantly less likely than the prison sample to be arrested. The difference between the shock graduate sample and the prison sample was not statistically significant.

Table 4.8
Results of Log-Normal Failure-Time Models Comparing Prison Releasee to Shock Graduate and Shock Dropout Samples in Florida Controlling for Age, Race, and Prior Conviction

	ARREST b (s.e.)[1]	ANY REVOCATION b (s.e.)	NEW CRIME REVOCATION b (s.e.)	TECHNICAL REVOCATION b (s.e.)
Shock Graduates[2]	0.38 (0.23)	0.56 (0.23)**	0.71 (0.30)**	0.27 (0.36)
Shock Dropouts[2]	0.69 (0.28)**	0.41 (0.27)	0.74 (0.37)**	-0.14 (0.39)
Age	0.22 (0.06)****	0.10 (0.24)*	0.15 (0.08)*	0.04 (0.08)
Race	0.36 (0.21)*	0.28 (0.21)	0.22 (0.26)	0.41 (0.32)
Prior Conviction	0.33 (0.25)	0.10 (0.24)	-0.08 (0.32)	0.34 (0.36)
Log-likelihood	-361.19	-160.99	-117.80	-77.09

*p<.10 **p<.05 ***p<.01 ****p<.001
[1] b (s.e.) represents the linear effect (and standard error) of the predictor variables on the log-normal transform of time to "failure," holding the other predictor variables constant.
[2] The prison sample is the reference sample. These coefficients represent the effect of being in the indicated sample compared to membership in the prison sample.

In sum, both the shock graduate and shock dropout samples consistently "outperformed" the prison sample. They failed at approximately the same rate, and controlling for demographic variables was generally significantly less likely to fail than the prison sample. Shock graduates and shock dropouts were therefore more similar to each other than to the prison comparison sample.

Georgia

Three samples (shock graduates, prison parolees, and probationers) were followed for two years in the community. Any revocation (including new crime, technical, and revocation due to absconding), new crime revocations, and technical revocations were examined. Lifetest analyses revealed significant differences among survival curves (see Tables 4.5 through 4.7). Both probation and prison samples appeared to fail at lower rates than the shock graduate sample. When demographic variables were controlled in the log-normal model, shock graduates were significantly more likely to be revoked in general and for a new crime than the probation sample (see Table 4.9). The shock graduate and prison samples did not differ significantly in the analysis of any revocations or new crime revocations. However, the shock graduate sample appeared to be slightly more likely to be revoked for a technical violation than the prison sample.

Table 4.9
Results of Log-Normal Failure-Time Models Comparing Probation to Shock Graduate and Releasee Samples in Georgia Controlling for Age, Race, and Prior Record

	ARREST b (s.e.)	ANY REVOCATION b (s.e.)[1]	NEW CRIME REVOCATION b (s.e.)	TECHNICAL REVOCATION b (s.e.)
Shock Graduates[2]	—	−0.08 (0.20)	−0.43 (0.22)**	−0.52 (0.64)
Prison[2]	—	0.37 (0.23)	−0.06 (0.25)	1.25 (0.86)
Age	—	0.05 (0.03)	0.07 (0.03)**	0.007(0.12)
Race	—	0.32 (0.16)**	0.10 (0.17)	0.23 (0.58)
Prior Record	—	1.01 (0.19)****	1.35 (0.20)****	1.12 (0.62)*
Log-likelihood	—	−243.42	−172.08	−53.10

*p<.10 **p<.05 ***p<.01 ****p<.001

[1] b (s.e.) represents the linear effect (and the standard error) of the predictor variables on the log-normal transform of time to "failure," holding the other predictor variables constant.

[2] The probation sample is the reference sample. These coefficients represent the effect of being in the indicated sample compared to membership in the probation sample.

Louisiana

Two shock graduate samples ("old" shock and "new" shock), one shock dropout sample, and samples of parolees and probationers were examined in Louisiana over a period of two years. Examination of Lifetest survival estimates, revealed that by and large old shock, new shock, and shock dropout samples failed at rather similar rates (see Tables 4.4 through 4.7). The prison and probation samples, too, failed at comparable rates. The Wilcoxon X^2

analyses, it appears that the new shock sample and the prison parolee sample are performing equivalently in the community. The probation-based samples, too, perform more similarly to each other than to either the new shock or prison samples.

What is seemingly inexplicable, however, is the fact that the prison-based offenders are "outperforming" the probation-based offenders, ostensibly the less serious offenders. An obvious answer to the question may be that performance on community supervision is a function of the intensity of supervision. In other words, offenders who are supervised intensively may be more likely to be caught than offenders who are less intensively supervised, despite the fact that both samples are committing infractions at the same rate upon release.

Table 4.11
Results of Log-Normal Failure-Time Models Comparing New Shock to Old Shock, Prison, Probation, and Split-Probation Samples in South Carolina Controlling for Age, Age-at-First Arrest, Race, and Prior Conviction

	ARREST b (s.e.)[1]	ANY REVOCATION b (s.e.)	NEW CRIME REVOCATION b (s.e.)	TECHNICAL REVOCATION b (s.e.)
Old Shock[2]	−0.72 (0.29)*	−1.63 (0.45)***	−1.51 (0.64)*	−1.79 (0.67)**
Prison[2]	−0.18 (0.31)	−0.67 (0.48)	−0.68 (0.68)	−0.67 (0.71)
Probation[2]	−0.34 (0.31)	−1.74 (0.47)***	−1.63 (0.66)*	−1.85 (0.69)**
Split-probation[2]	−1.11 (0.44)*	−1.87 (0.62)**	−1.41 (0.99)	−2.19 (0.85)**
Age	0.10 (0.73)	0.09 (0.09)	0.36 (0.17)*	−0.06 (0.12)
Age-1st-Arrest	0.08 (0.08)	0.11 (0.11)	−0.15 (0.17)	0.26 (0.15)*
Race	0.82 (0.22)***	0.57 (0.27)*	0.50 (0.37)	0.71 (0.39)*
Prior Conviction	0.28 (0.24)	0.30 (0.29)	0.87 (0.44)*	−0.09 (0.41)
Log-likelihood	−396.96	−182.47	−98.96	−119.39

*p<.05   **p<.01   ***p<.001

[1] b (s.e.) represents the linear effect (and standard error) of the predictor variables on the log-normal transform of time to "failure," holding the other predictor variables constant.

[2] The new shock graduate sample is the reference sample. These coefficients represent the effect of being in the indicated sample compared to membership in the new shock graduate sample.

Based on interviews with state officials, this in fact appears to be at least partially true. South Carolina Department of Probation, Parole, and Pardon Services records indicate that approximately 51 percent (N=699) of the total number of shock incarceration graduates prior to the legislative change had been intensively supervised. Since the control of the program shifted to the DOC, only .2 percent (N=1) of the total number of new shock graduates had received intensive supervision upon release. As a matter of practice, inmates released from the new shock program receive intensive supervision only if judicially ordered. Supervision intensity may therefore explain the differences in recidivism between old shock and new shock samples. It does not, however, explain why the new shock and prison parolee samples were significantly less likely to fail than the probation-based samples because probationers were also most likely to be placed on regular supervision caseloads. Approximately, 10 percent (N=1,523) of the probationers admitted to probation during the 1989-1990 fiscal year (the year of data collection) were intensively supervised.

CONCLUSION

Do shock incarceration programs reduce recidivism? An unqualified response seems premature. The results of the present evaluation were inconsistent across states and did not permit a conclusive answer. To some extent, this should be expected given the fact that the programs themselves differ considerably in the type of offender selected for participation, the selection process, the nature of program activities, and the intensity of community supervision (see Appendix A). Due to legislative mandates or changes in policy, individual programs, too, tend to change over time. For this reason, two samples of shock graduates were selected in both Louisiana and South Carolina.

At first glance, there does appear to be some promising evidence in support of the efficacy of shock incarceration programs. In Florida, for example, shock graduates were significantly less likely to be revoked in general and to be revoked for new crimes compared with the sample of offenders released from prison. In Louisiana, new shock graduates were also significantly less likely to be revoked for a new crime than prison parolees and shock dropouts.

In South Carolina, the sample of new shock graduates "outperformed" two probation-based samples as well as a sample of old shock graduates. While the influence of supervision intensity cannot be discounted, the fact remains that new shock graduates failed at approximately the same rate as did prison parolees supervised at equivalent intensity levels. In Georgia, too, the performance of shock graduates and prison parolees did not differ once demographic variables were controlled.

On the basis of the Florida and Louisiana results, it might be tempting to conclude that the shock incarceration experience has a beneficial effect on recidivism, reducing the likelihood of revocation for new crimes. It might further be argued that the increased likelihood of revocation for a technical violation in Louisiana is probably attributable to the six months of intense supervision required of the shock graduates. In both states, there were no significant differences among samples when arrest was examined as the outcome measure.

Absent the examination of samples of shock incarceration dropouts, this may have been a reasonable conclusion. However, the striking similarity between shock graduates and shock dropouts, particularly in Florida, casts increased threat to public safety as a result of a reduced term of imprisonment. However, there is no evidence that the shock incarceration experience in and of itself had an impact on behavior during community supervision.

A PENDIX A

FLORIDA

In 1987, the Florida Depart ent of Corrections (DOC) implemented a shock incarceration program. In o 'er to participate in the program, offenders must be sentenced under the You ful Offender Act (YOA) or designated a youthful offender by the DOC unde the same act (Florida DOC, 1989). In both instances, offenders must additionall meet the following program eligibility criteria: (1) no previous incarcerations in a state or federal facility; (2) male less than 24 years of age; and (3) servir g a sentence of 10 years or less for other than a capital or life felony (Florid OC, 1989). Further, eligible offenders cannot have any physical or mental itations that would preclude full participation in strenuous physical acti y. The Florida DOC may also screen offenders based on criminal history.

Florida operates one shock pro n that houses up to 100 inmates. Offenders spend an average of 3.3 mo (90 to 120 days) in the shock program. The program is located within rger correctional facility; however, offenders are housed separately fro general population inmates. Upon release from shock, offenders receive gular supervision in the community.

GEORGIA

Georgia's shock incarceration program called the Special Alternative Incarceration Program (SAIP) was one of the first boot camp programs to become operational nationwide in 1983 (Flowers, Carr & Ruback, 1991). Developed to target young and less serious offenders, eligibility criteria include: (1) male between 17 and 25 years of age at sentencing; (2) conviction of a felony; (3) sentence length of at least one year; and (4) no previous period of incarceration in an adult penal institution. Offenders have to be assessed for eligibility prior to receiving a judicial order to the program and are sentenced to the program as a condition of probation.

At the time of this study, Georgia operated two boot camp prison programs housing approximately 150 inmates each. Offenders spend three months in the program. Upon release, graduates are returned to court and are generally placed on probation. However, shock graduates may also be placed on intensive probation supervision or sent to a diversion center. Those who are dismissed from the shock incarceration program for misbehavior or other problems that preclude participation (e.g., medical condition) must return to the court to be resentenced. During its first six years of operation (when it was selected for participation in the multi-site study), Georgia's programs were easily distinguishable from many other shock programs due to their almost exclusive focus on work detail. Subsequent to multi-site data collection (in 1989), increased emphasis has been placed on treatment-oriented activities during the course of the program.

LOUISIANA

Louisiana's shock incarceration program, called IMPACT (Intensive Motivational Program of Alternative Correctional Treatment), is a two-phase program that consists of a period of 90 to 180 days (on average 120 days) of incarceration followed by a minimum of six months of intensive parole supervision (LDPSC, 1987). Program eligibility criteria include the following: (1) conviction of an offense that carries parole eligibility; (2) conviction of a first felony offense; (3) commitment to the Department of Public Safety and Corrections for seven years or less; (4) recommendation for IMPACT by the Division of Probation and Parole (in a presentence investigation report, if recommendation is part of initial sentencing rather than probation revocation proceedings); (5) recommendation for IMPACT by the sentencing court; (6) recommendation for IMPACT by a screening committee at the IMPACT site; and (7) willingness of offender to enroll. Otherwise legally eligible offenders are denied entry into the program based on the following list of suitability criteria: (1) age of 40 years or older; (2) pending undisposed felony or misdemeanor charges; (3) conviction of a sex offense against children or sex offense accompanied by violent behavior (sex offenders who have committed less serious sex offenses are not automa˙ ˙ally excluded); (4) conviction of felony DWI (third offense); (5) a men˙   ˙hysical health problem that would preclude full participation in institut   ˙ck or in a subsequent period of intensive c˙ ˙munity supervision; (6)   ˙istory revealing significant, long-ter˙ ˙istory of violent behavior; a˙˙   (7) overt homosexuality. Since th˙ ˙me of multi-site data collection, the ˙   bility criteria have been slightly r˙vised.

Offend˙.s may be discharged for misbehavior, poor ˳ ˙gress, or medical/psychological problems. In addition, they may volun˙ ˙rily request to leave. R˙gardless of the reason, they are required to serve ˙˙e remainder of their sentence in a traditional prison until paroled by the parol˙ board. Those who successfully complete the program are paroled and begin in˙ensive supervision in the community.

SOUTH CAROLINA

Shock incarceration, formerly called shock probation in South ˙ ˙olina, was developed as part of the Omnibus Criminal Justice Improvemen˙   t of fer significantly on any of the variables except age upon release and offense type. The prison comparison sample was significantly older than the shock dropout sample.

Instruments and Procedure

The record data and Offender Adjustment to Community Supervis n instrument described in the general methodology section were used. ' ie "record data" questionnaire was completed by Florida site researchers. he Offender Adjustment to Community Supervision instrument was comple/ 1 at three-month intervals over the course of one year by supervisory agents. OC researchers mailed the questionnaire to supervisory agents every three months. The first survey was completed at the end of approximatel three months of community supervision.

GEORGIA METHODOLOGY

Subjects

The following three samples were evaluated: (1) a shock arceration graduate sample (N=79); (2) a sample of prison releasees (N=( )); and (3) a sample of probationers (N=85). There were too few dropouts o follow as a sample. Due to transfers out of state or early release from su iervision, final sample sizes did not equal 100.

Shock Graduate Sample. The Georgia DOC database w s used to select the shock graduate sample. One hundred offenders were /an^omly selected from a computer-generated list of shock graduates who wer ,eing released to community supervision.

Probationer and Parolee Samples. The Georgia DOC database was used to generate a list of probationers and parolees who met all shock eligibility criteria. One hundred parolees and probationers were then randomly selected to be included in each sample.

Sample Demographic Comparisons

Analyses of demographic variables revealed that samples differed significantly on age and offense type (see Table 4.1). Prison releasees were significantly older at release than both the shock graduate and probation samples. Samples also differed significantly in terms of offense type. A larger percentage of the shock graduate and prison samples were convicted of robbery than the probation sample while a larger percentage of the probation and prison samples were convicted of a drug offense. Indicators of criminal history were not included in the analysis because they were of questionable validity due to the data collection process.

Instruments and Procedure

The record data instrument described in the general methodology section was completed by Georgia DOC researchers. Although the Offender Adjustment to Community Supervision instrument was completed at three-month intervals by supervisory agents for a total period of 1 year, preliminary analysis revealed questionable and sometimes implausible dates. Therefore, researchers validated the data collected by the Offender Adjustment to Community Supervision instrument using the Georgia DOC computer database. Due to this method of data collection, only revocations for either new crimes, technical violations, or absconding were recorded. (Reliable arrest data was not available for all subjects therefore it was not analyzed.) Samples, however, were tracked for two years of community supervision.

LOUISIANA METHODOLOGY

Subjects

Five samples were compared in this study: two samples of shock incarceration inmates (old shock sample (N=102), new shock sample (N=117)); a prison releasee sample (N=143); a sample of probationers (N=108); and a sample of shock dropouts (N=72).

Old Shock Sample. The old shock sample consisted of all male graduates of the shock incarceration program who entered the program between October 1987 and October 1988.

New Shock Sample. The new shock sample consisted of all male graduates of the shock incarceration program who graduated from the program between May 1989 and March 1990. Due to differences in selection procedures that had been relaxed in order to increase the number of offenders entering the program, it was hypothesized that the new shock sample might have been composed of more serious offenders.

Probation Sample. Subjects included in the probation sample met the shock program eligibility requirements. In addition, they received a primary recommendation for the shock program by a probation agent.

Parole Sample. Regular population inmates who were paroled between October 1987 and October 1988 were selected for participation in the parole sample. The dockets for parole hearings were examined to identify first-time offenders. Possible candidates were then identified at the probation and parole district office. Three probation and parole employees volunteered to review the records and decide whether offenders might have been recommended for the shock program. Cases receiving two or three votes for a positive shock recommendation were included in the sample.

Shock Incarceration Dropout Sample. The shock dropout sample was made up of offenders who entered the program between October 1987 and October 1988 and failed to graduate. Dropouts served the remainder of their sentence in a traditional prison until eligible for parole.

Sample Demographic Comparisons

Demographic comparisons revealed that samples differed significantly in terms of age at release and criminal history variables (see Table 4.2). The prison releasee sample was significantly older than all of the other samples by at least two years. A greater percentage of old shock graduates, new shock graduates, and shock dropouts had a criminal history and were previously incarcerated than the prison releasee and probation comparisons samples.

Instruments and Procedure

The Louisiana study served as a model for the multi-site study of shock incarceration. Therefore, the instruments were slightly different. The data collected was more extensive and therefore allowed comparisons to be drawn between Louisiana and the other participating sites. An instrument very similar to the Offender Adjustment to Community Supervision was used to collect recidivism data. Researchers used the instrument to collect data on each subject from records kept at district probation and parole offices. Data were collected at one point in time, between April and June, 1991.

SOUTH CAROLINA METHODOLOGY

Subjects

Five samples of male offenders were compared during community supervision. The samples included: (1) a sample of shock program graduates (old shock) who completed the program prior to legislative changes in the state that shifted control of the program from the Probation, Parole, and Pardon Services to the DOC (N=85); (2) a sample of shock program graduates who completed the program after the legislative change (new shock) (N=84); (3) a sample of probationers (N=69); (4) a sample of split-probationers (N=24); and (5) a sample of prison releasees sentenced under the Youth Offender Act (N=64). A sample of shock dropouts was not examined due to an insufficient number of shock program dropouts to constitute a sample.

Old Shock Sample. The sample was selected randomly from a database of shock incarceration graduates. All subjects graduated from the program between October and December 1989 when the program was under the supervision of Probation, Parole, and Pardon Services.

New Shock Sample. Four consecutive classes of shock graduates who entered the program between January and March 1991 were selected. Program control shifted to the DOC in June 1990 in order to maximize the ability of the program to reduce prison crowding. It was expected that offenders chosen for participation in shock from a pool of offenders sentenced to the DOC would be more likely to have otherwise served time in prison.

Probation Sample. The probation sample was randomly selected from probationers who met shock incarceration legal eligibility criteria and began supervision between October and December 1989.

Split-Probation Sample. The split-probation sample was initially selected as part of the probation sample. After selection and data collection, it was discovered that they had served a short period of time in prison by virtue of a split-probation sentence. They were therefore analyzed as a separate sample.

Prison Parolee. The prison parolee sample was randomly selected from parolees who met shock incarceration legal eligibility criteria and were released to parole between October and December 1989.

Sample Demographic Comparisons

Analyses revealed that samples differed significantly on all demographic comparisons (see Table 4.2). Split-probationers were significantly older than all of the other samples upon release to community supervision. The probation sample was significantly older at first arrest than both samples of shock incarceration graduates as well as the prison releasee sample. The samples also differed significantly in terms of race, criminal history, and offense type. A greater percentage of the new shock sample had been previously arrested, for example, but greater percentages of the split-probation and prison samples had been previously convicted.

Instruments and Procedure

Researchers in South Carolina collected demographic information using the record data instrument. The Offender Adjustment to Community Supervision instrument was completed by supervisory agents at three-month intervals for a period of one year for all samples except the new shock graduate sample. Supervisory agents completed the Offender Adjustment to Community Supervision instrument for the new shock sample at one point in time after one full year of community supervision.

the level of priority given to program elements of SI programs?; (3) How well do articulated goals for programs as espoused by system level officials parallel those perceived to exist by individuals responsible for the delivery of services?; (4) Do goal statements and program priorities of more recently opened programs indicate greater concern with the rehabilitative/behavior change of offenders than those associated with older programs?; (5) What is the contemporary nature of drug treatment programming in boot camps?

LITERATURE REVIEW

Shock Incarceration Goals

According to Parent (1989) and Osler (1991), incapacitation, rehabilitation, retribution, and deterrence are all commonly espoused goals of SI programs. However, these traditional aims of the correctional sanction have not been used systematically to understand the motivations behind the emergence of boot camps or the decisions to employ particular program models.

In January 1990, 7 of the 14 states operating SI programs were chosen to participate in a multi-site study sponsored by the National Institute of Justice. These programs were selected due to the similarities they exhibited in regard to characteristics (e.g., all programs operated through a boot camp atmosphere with strict rules and discipline) that were used to define such programs. One purpose of this research was to ascertain whether SI programs were successful in attaining their stated goals. MacKenzie's work (1990) in this area presents a clearly defined and specified group of goals that apply to specific individuals or groups that are directly affected by SI programs; the correctional system, the offender, the public, and the individual correctional facilities. From interviews and official agency documents, the following goals were identified (MacKenzie, 1990):

SYSTEM-LEVEL GOALS
Reduce Crowding
Alternative to Longer-term Incarceration
Less Cost
Model for County Programs

PUBLIC RELATIONS GOALS
Improve Image of Corrections
Politically Acceptable Alternative
Public Safety

PRISON CONTROL/ MANAGEMENT GOALS
Clean, Healthy, Secure Environment
Environment Promoting Rehabilitation
Positive Offender/Staff Contact
Offender Accountability

INDIVIDUAL-LEVEL GOALS
Change Offenders—Less Negative Behavior & Less Criminal Activity
Change Offenders—More Positive Attitudes/Behavior
Improve Confidence and Responsibilty
Discipline
Motivation
Positive Social Values
Positive Social Behavior (e.g., Work Ethic)
Reduce Drug Use
Accountability
Respect for Authority

Among the seven states, MacKenzie and colleagues reported that there was a high consistency among the targeted system-level goals specified. All goals associated within the system-level, with the exception of the program to be used as a model for county programs, were commonly identified. Individual-level goals were also reported by the majority of states, however specific goals varied between states. The public relations goals were listed only by a few states, and when mentioned, the goal of improving the image of corrections was most commonly identified. Finally, only one of the seven states listed goals related to prison control/management as purposes of their SI program(s) (MacKenzie, 1990).

In 1992, an additional survey was conducted by MacKenzie to obtain up-to-date information on the goals of shock incarceration programs. However, the multi-target goal classification (i.e., system-level, individual-level, public relations, and prison control/management) previously developed was not used. Instead, as seen below, the goal selections made available to program respondents included a mix of core system aims, multi-target group goals, and programs elements.

CORE SYSTEM AIMS
Rehabilitation
Deterrence
Punishment/Retribution

MULTI-TARGET GROUP AIMS
Reduce Recidivism
Reduce Crowding
Safe Prison Environment

PROGRAM ELEMENTS
Drug Education
Work Skills
Vocational Education
Drug Treatment
Education

A sample of 41 administrators who were responsible for developing and/or overseeing the boot camps were asked to rate the relative importance of these 11 possible program goals. Rehabilitation, recidivism reduction, drug education, and the reduction of prison crowding were ranked the highest by respondents. Vocational education and punishment were identified as less important goals (Elis, MacKenzie & Souryal, unpublished).

When discussing what is to be achieved by SI programs, a distinction should be made between program *goals* and program *elements*. Five of the 11 goals listed by Elis, MacKenzie, and Souryal (unpublished) are generally considered to be program elements—activities in which offenders participate—rather than program goals. That is, these program elements are the means rather than the ends of SI. Furthermore, three of the remaining six goals are core system aims that can be considered to be broader constructs subsuming more narrowly defined correctional goals (e.g., rehabilitation includes reduced recidivism).

This review of the goals of SI programs indicates that a wide number of goals seem to characterize such programming. Unfortunately, attempts to measure goal orientations at different points in time have utilized differing goal definitions and questionable goal classifications. This makes it difficult to trace how goal structures may have changed over time.

Evolution of Program Elements

The program content of early boot camps was generally consistent across facilities. It included a military design in which offenders participated in physical training, drill and ceremony, and hard labor (MacKenzie, 1990; Coyle, 1990; MacKenzie, in press). As these programs were developed, basic rehabilitative elements such as substance abuse treatment and education (although commonly present) were overshadowed by the strong emphasis on structure and discipline.

According to Sechrest (1989:20), SI programs may be successful for certain inmates if ". . . they [SI programs] can be expanded to include education, job training, and skill development components starting in the facility and continuing into the community." Similarly, Osler (1991), remarked that while SI programs were successful in "tearing down" the inmate, they released the offender before he could be "rebuilt." He claimed that these programs were not of sufficient duration to produce successful offender outcomes.

Correctional system officials responsible for SI programming in some states have acknowledged these concerns. For example, Florida officials conceded that for some inmates ". . . these unmet needs [substance abuse treatment and education, basic education, and job training] . . . may have negated any rehabilitative success in other areas" (Florida Department of Corrections, 1990:25). In a 1991 evaluation of Georgia's Special Alternative Incarceration (SAI) program, the necessity of enhanced substance abuse programming was also highlighted:

> At least three-quarters of the offenders who have gone through SAI have a problem with drugs and/or alcohol. They committed crimes while under the influence or to support their habits, or they were convicted of DUI or drug possession or sale. Strong substance abuse programs were needed, both in SAI and during the follow-up period of supervision and treatment. (Georgia Department of Corrections, 1991:XI). It thus became recognized that little evidence existed to support the idea that discipline and hard work, by themselves, would lead to long-lasting behavioral changes.

In addition to the lack of emphasis placed on standard rehabilitative elements within the boot camp environment, concern about the lack of aftercare services, especially for the substance abusing client, has been voiced as programs have grown in popularity. For example, in a study that examined the post-release experiences of boot camp inmates from Louisiana, Shaw, and MacKenzie (1991:63) note that:

> . . . the behavior of problem drinkers as a group was more varied than that of non-problem drinkers, emphasizing the importance of and the need for programs such as this [Shock Incarceration] to provide adequate support and aftercare for problem drinkers and substance abusers.

Thus, since the initial introduction of SI programs there appears to have been considerable modification in the structuring of programs. While early shock incarceration programs emphasized structure and discipline, newer programs appear to be incorporating more substance abuse treatment into daily inmate programming and a stronger post-release aftercare component. It is assumed that these changes in the structuring of programs reflect alterations in previously elaborated goals. However, available data are not adequate for us to know the extent to which this is true. In the following pages, the methodology used to acquire relevant data on these issues is presented, as are the findings that inform our understanding of shock incarceration goals and program elements.

METHODOLOGY

A variety of survey techniques were utilized in the present research, which is part of a study sponsored by the National Institute of Justice to collect information on the nature of drug treatment and aftercare programming offered among the universe of adult shock incarceration programs. SI programs were operationalized "as any program labeled a Shock Incarceration program by a sponsoring correctional agency, which includes a training component not necessarily based on a military model, and is an incarceration—based alternative to a traditional prison sentence." This broad definition allowed for the inclusion in this study of programs that do not use a paramilitary model. The research goal was to identify and survey the universe of federal and state SI programs for adult offenders.

Data were collected in two stages. The first stage was directed towards the person at the system level most directly responsible for the planning, implementation, or oversight of SI programming. The second stage was directed towards the site-level administrator and substance abuse treatment/education

facility administrators, and individuals responsible for the delivery of substance abuse education and/or treatment at boot camp facilities. In this table, only system-level officials from jurisdictions in which a substance abuse questionnaire was returned are included to ensure the direct comparability of responses across individuals who work in the same set of correctional systems (n=22).

The means presented in Tables 5.1 and 5.2 for system-level officials are remarkably similar. For instance, the mean score for rehabilitation as a cor-

Table 5.2
Ratings of the Importance of Correctional Aims and Goals for Shock Incarceration Facilities as Reported by System-Level Officials,[a] Site-Level Administrators, and Site-Level Substance Abuse Treatment/Education Providers

	System Level Respondents (n=22)		Facility Administrators (n=23)		Substance Abuse Treatment/ Education Providers (n=25)	
	Mean	S.D	Mean	S.D.	Mean	S.D.
CORRECTIONAL AIMS:						
Retribution	3.45	.69	3.65	1.00	3.56	1.10
Incapacitation	2.91	1.04	3.06	1.21	3.00	1.11
Rehabilitation	1.43	.68	1.29	.56	1.48	.79
Deterrence	2.19	.87	2.60	.82	2.41	.85
GOALS[b]:						
SYSTEM LEVEL:						
Reduce Crowding	2.64	1.65	2.61	1.83	2.88	1.83
Improve Image of Corrections	3.59	1.47	4.09	1.98	3.08	1.58
Public Safety	1.68	1.04	2.04	1.36	1.72	.84
Alternative to Longer-Term Incarceration	1.50	.91	1.78	1.24	1.76	1.27
Less Cost	2.23	.97	2.57	1.75	2.00	1.00
Politically Acceptable Alternative to Prison	2.41	.96	3.30	1.64	3.16	1.84
Model for County Programs	5.64	2.22	4.52	2.00	4.28	1.86
INDIVIDUAL LEVEL:						
Instill Respect for Authority	1.55	.74	1.26	.54	1.12	.33
Promoting Discipline	1.64	.85	1.39	.78	1.08	.28
Less Criminal Activity	1.86	.83	2.39	1.41	1.96	1.14
Improve Confidence	2.05	1.21	1.65	.83	1.88	1.20
Reduce Drug Use	2.41	1.30	1.39	.66	1.52	.77
Positive Social Behaviors	2.00	1.07	1.52	.67	1.64	.91
PRISON CONTROL/MANAGEMENT:						
Clean, Healthy Environment	2.36	1.14	1.48	1.04	1.36	.57
Offender Accountability	2.05	1.40	1.87	1.74	1.76	1.01
Positive Offender/Staff Contact	2.23	1.19	1.91	.95	2.36	1.41
Environment Promoting Rehabilitation	1.77	.92	1.52	.90	1.68	.99

[a]In this table, only system-level respondents for jurisdictions with returned site-level substance abuse questionnaires are included (22 of 31 total).
[b]Means of goals are based on a scale of 1 (very important goal) to 7 (goal not important at all).

rectional aim and the array of scores associated with program goals (e.g., public safety, alternative to long-term incarceration, instill respect for authority, reduce drug use) are very comparable in terms of both magnitude and relative ranks. Thus, it appears that the subset of facilities that generated returned questionnaires are very similar to the universe of adult boot camps in terms of system-level stated program aims and goals, suggesting a minimal level of response bias in the pattern of questionnaire returns.

Table 5.2 indicates that there is a strong level of agreement as to the aims and goals of boot camps across system-level officials, facility administrators, and officials in charge of delivering substance abuse treatment and education to SI participants. For instance, each group gives primacy to rehabilitation as a correctional aim of the boot camp, with deterrence, incapacitation, and retribution being emphasized in decreasing order. Further, each group of respondents ranks alternatives to longer-term incarceration, public safety, and lower cost as the top three system-level goals of boot camps in the same order although the mean scores for facility administrators are slightly higher (less priority attached) than for the other respondent types.

Interestingly, more notable variation in rankings across respondent types is found among the individual-level goals. While each group ranked instilling respect for authority and promoting discipline as the primary individual-level goals of their SI facility, facility-level administrators did not rank the reduction of criminal activity as highly as did system-officials. Conversely, system-level officials ranked reduced drug use as the least important individual-level goal (mean of 2.41) while facility staff ranked reduced drug use much more highly (mean of 1.39 and 1.52), and at a level more comparable to those given promoting discipline and instilling respect for authority. Facility-based staff also gave higher rankings in general to most of the prison control/management goals than did system-level officials, perhaps reflecting their immediate work environments and the emphasis given order and accountability within such environments.

Despite the slight differences noted above across respondent types, in general there is a high level of agreement between system officials, facility administrators, and facility drug treatment/education supervisors as to the aims and goals of SI facilities. Rehabilitation as the primary aim of such facilities and an emphasis on instilling respect for authority and promoting discipline are consensual themes in the data. There is some variation placed on the goal of reducing drug use, with facility-based staff placing greater emphasis on this goal than system-level administrators.

Table 5.3 presents the responses of all three respondent types as to whether their SI facility incorporates particular program elements into their overall programming efforts.

Table 5.3

The Percentage of Facilities in Which Various Elements Exist as Reported by System-Level Officials,[a] Site-Level Administrators, and Site-Level Substance Treatment Providers

ELEMENTS	System-Level Officials (n=22)	Site-Level Administrators (n=23)	Site Level Substance Abuse Treatment Education Providers (n=25)
	%	%	%
Physical Training	100	96	96
Alcohol Treatment	100	87	76
Drug Treatment	100	87	76
Substance Abuse Education	100	100	100
Physical Labor	100	100	100
Drill/Ceremony	100	100	100
Basic Education	95	87	100
Vocational Education	41	30	44
Pre-Release Programming	95	96	96
Post-Release Services Delivery	77	78	68

[a]In this table, only system-level respondents for jurisdictions with a returned site-level substance abuse questionnaire are included (22 of 31 total).

All respondents indicated that substance abuse education, physical labor, and drill/ceremony are program elements in their facility. The vast bulk of respondents also indicated that physical training, basic education, and pre-release programming are facility program components. Conversely, vocational education is not commonly found in SI facilities. Only slightly more than 40 percent of the system-level and site-level substance abuse treatment/education providers indicated that vocational education is a facility program element. Notably, only 30 percent of site-level administrators similarly responded.

This last finding illustrates that discrepancies occur when differing categories of individuals are asked about whether particular program elements exist in SI facilities. This issue is most manifest when attention turns to alcohol and drug treatment programming.

All system-level respondents indicated that alcohol and drug treatment services are being provided in their SI facility. However, 13 percent (n=3) of the site level administrators and 24 percent (n=6) of the site-level substance abuse treatment/education providers indicated that no alcohol or drug treatment is being provided. Thus, there appears to be considerable confusion among some respondents as to whether there is even a drug treatment program in existence at certain facilities. Disagreement even appears at the same facility. At one facility, the site-level administrator indicated that drug treatment was given moderate priority while the individual supposedly responsible for the delivery of substance abuse services indicated there was no such programming at the facility.

Table 5.4 presents mean priority ranking scores for particular program elements across respondent types. These scores reflect only those responses in which it was indicated that a particular program element was part of overall facility programming. For instance, the mean score of 3.56 for vocational education (on a scale of 1 to 6) among system-level officials is based on respondents who stated that such a program element is in place (41% of the total). In general, this table reveals considerably more variation across respondent types in the priority attached to program elements than in the priorities attached to program aims and goals.

Table 5.4
Ratings of the Importance of Program Elements[a] for Shock Incarceration Facilities as Reported by System-Level Officials,[b] Site-Level Administrators, and Site-Level Substance Abuse Treatment Providers

	System-Level Officials (n=22)		Site-Level Administrators (n=23)		Site-Level Substance Abuse Treatment/Education Providers (n=25)	
ELEMENTS[c]	Mean	S.D.	Mean	S.D.	Mean	S.D.
Physical Training	1.64	1.05	1.68	1.17	1.13	.45
Alcohol Treatment	2.36	1.10	1.30	.73	1.53	1.02
Drug Treatment	2.32	1.17	1.30	.73	1.47	1.02
Substance Abuse Education	1.96	1.00	1.30	.64	1.88	1.20
Physical Labor	1.91	1.41	1.87	1.33	1.96	1.43
Drill/Ceremony	1.68	.89	1.83	1.19	1.52	.65
Basic Education	2.67	1.39	2.40	1.60	2.44	1.47
Vocational Education	3.56	1.51	3.86	1.68	3.82	1.83
Pre-Release Programming	2.81	1.47	1.55	.91	2.00	1.45
Post-Release Services Delivery	2.18	1.29	2.44	1.50	2.41	1.81

[a]Elements identified by respondents as not being a program element were excluded from calculations of mean scores.
[b]In this table, only system-level respondents for jurisdictions with a returned site-level substance abuse questionnaire are included (22 of 31 total).
[c]Means of elements are based on a scale of 1 (primary program element) to 6 (minor program element).

Among system-level officials, elements traditionally associated with military-style boot camps: physical training, drill and ceremony, and physical labor are consistently rated high. However, traditional rehabilitative program-

"Older" versus "Newer" Shock Facilities

MacKenzie (in press), among others, has indicated that newer shock facilities are incorporating more therapy and treatment into the daily schedule of the programs than did earlier shock programs. To assess whether this is true, and to determine if these changes reflect modified goal structures among more recent programs, Table 5.5 presents the mean rankings for correctional aims, goals, and priority given program elements as reported by site-level administrators for programs that became operational before June, 1990 (n=12), and those that become operational after June, 1990 (n=11).

Table 5.5 indicates that there is very little difference in the rankings attributed to correctional aims by site-level administrators of older and newer facilities. Both groups endorse rehabilitation very strongly. System-level goals are emphasized a bit differently among the respondents. Newer facilities are more oriented to being an alternative to longer-term incarceration and to saving the system money than are older facilities. Little difference is found with regard to prison control/management goals other than newer facilities emphasizing an environment that promotes rehabilitation more so than older facilities. More notable differences are found with regard to individual-level goals. Administrators of newer facilities report that reducing drug use and promoting positive social behaviors are more prominent goals of their facilities than those reported by administrators of older facilities.

These differences are clearly apparent when the priority given specific program elements is examined. Administrators of older facilities report higher rankings attached to vocational education, physical labor, and drill and ceremony than do administrators of newer facilities. The latter officials report higher rankings for all other program elements than do the former officials, with differences being pronounced for alcohol and drug treatment (1.60 to 1.00), pre-release programming (1.82 to 1.27), and post-release service delivery (3.11 to 1.78).

These data suggest that more recently opened facilities appear to be taking less of a militaristic approach with their clients, emphasizing to a greater degree the provision of treatment and services commonly thought to address basic offender needs (e.g., drug and alcohol problems) which are thought to make the transition to the free world community easier and more crime-free (e.g., pre-release programming and aftercare services).

THE NATURE OF SUBSTANCE ABUSE PROGRAMMING

Thus far, discussion has focused on the perceptions of correctional officials at the system and facility levels regarding the nature of correctional aims, goals, and program elements of SI programs. In this section, the focus is on presenting an overview of substance abuse treatment and/or education programming in SI facilities.

The Treatment Decision

Of the 25 SI facilities from which an individual designated as providing substance abuse services responded to the questionnaire, slightly more than three-quarters (n=19) have a substance abuse program. Of that number, nearly 85 percent (n=16), require substance abuse treatment of all shock incarceration participants, while another 10 percent (n=2) require "certain" offenders, such as those with substance abuse histories and those with conviction offenses involving drugs, to participate in substance abuse programs. Only one of the 19 boot camp programs providing substance abuse treatment makes the treatment available on a purely voluntary basis.

The decision that an individual requires substance abuse treatment is most frequently considered in the free world community to be one that should be a clinical determination rather than a legal one. In many instances within boot camps, this does not appear to be the situation. Of the 19 identified boot camps providing treatment, slightly more than one-third (7 facilities, 36.80%) worked within a statutory requirement mandating treatment of boot camp clients. Additionally, two facilities indicated that the sentencing judge mandated treatment, while three sites stated that it was mandated by the facility without a substance abuse assessment. Four more programs indicated that treatment was mandated upon assessment by the facility, and an additional two identified other avenues that compelled treatment. Thus, mandated client participation in SI drug treatment programming is most often based on factors not necessarily associated with clinical judgments of need, amenability, or potential effectiveness.

Assessment of Substance Abuse Problems

Most of the facilities surveyed indicated that they conduct a substance abuse assessment of their participants. Seventeen of the 25 sites responding to the questionnaire indicated some type of assessment process was utilized. Interestingly, two states that have assessment processes do not provide substance abuse treatment at the facility level. One facility indicated that it had previously operated a treatment program but had moved to a substance abuse education only regimen; it continued the assessment process nonetheless. Another site indicated that it provided substance abuse education but not treatment, and that an assessment was done for purposes of individualizing aftercare treatment plans.

As can be seen in Figure 5.1 a variety of assessment techniques were identified by the respondents. By far the most commonly used assessment tool was a face-to-face interview (94% with about half utilizing a Structured

Interview Format from the DSM-III-R). About 75 percent of the facilities also indicated that they used behavioral or psychological tests and an equal percentage (75%) used case histories that went beyond the individual's offense history. Although a variety of tests appear to be used by the boot camps, the most frequently specified were the Michigan Alcoholism Screening Test (MAST), used by half of the those employing assessment tests, and the Inventory of Drinking Situations, used by slightly more than one-third (37.5%) of those engaging in client assessment.

Figure 5.1
Type of Substance Abuse Assessment Used by Boot Camps

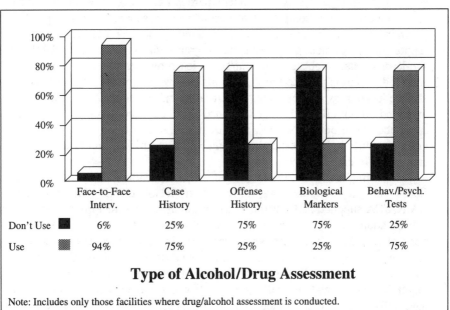

	Face-to-Face Interv.	Case History	Offense History	Biological Markers	Behav./Psych. Tests
Don't Use	6%	25%	75%	75%	25%
Use	94%	75%	25%	25%	75%

Type of Alcohol/Drug Assessment

Note: Includes only those facilities where drug/alcohol assessment is conducted.

In line with the mandatory nature of most substance abuse programming discussed above, about 65 percent (*n*=11) of the facilities utilizing assessment techniques reported that data collected from assessment were not used to classify inmates for treatment programming. Respondents from only six programs indicated that the assessment information was used for treatment classification. One SI program reported that a rather extensive assessment process was employed including face-to-face interviews, case history reviews, and behavioral/psychological testing assessment (five different assessment tests were used). Further, the program utilized the DSM-III-R classification system. Paradoxically, this program stated that this extensive assessment was not used to classify inmates or direct them into substance abuse treatment. Rather ". . .

all inmates are required to be in treatment as a condition of acceptance into the program." Thus, it appears that many shock incarceration facilities do engage in assessment efforts but the results often bear little clinical relevance to the treatment offered.

Treatment Modalities and Interventions

Echoing the general diversity found among individual SI facilities in other areas, there is a wide range in the types of treatments offered by the facilities. The most commonly identified treatment "modality" was substance abuse education, which was identified by 17 of the 19 facilities offering substance abuse treatment. Differing respondent perceptions as to whether substance abuse education is a component of treatment or a separate and independent program element obscures a clear understanding of how educational efforts support or complement drug treatment programming in SI facilities. All 25 SI site-level substance abuse treatment/education providers stated that substance abuse education is provided to their inmates. Five programs include substance abuse education as a component of their larger substance abuse treatment regimen and do not offer a distinct substance abuse education program, 14 utilize substance abuse education both as a treatment modality and a distinct program element, and six respondents indicated that only substance abuse education is offered.

Following education, the next most frequent treatment modalities identified were group counseling, provided at 16 of the 19 facilities, and AA/NA/CA supplied at 15 of the 19 SI programs. Milieu therapy and individualized counseling programs were provided by about two-thirds of the facilities—at 13 and 12 of the sites, respectively. The least used treatment modality was the therapeutic community, found only in 2 of the 19 programs. To explore the possibility that the nature of treatment modalities provided might be constrained by staffing levels (for e.g., some facilities might not have sufficient staff to provide individual counseling and as a result use less staff-intensive modalities such as AA/NA or group counseling) ratios for treatment staff to inmates across facilities with differing treatment modalities were calculated. The differences in staffing levels for the various modalities did not support this notion. Mean staffing ratios ranged from a high of 16.5 inmates per staff member in facilities that had group counseling to a low of just under 13 inmates per treatment staff member in facilities that utilized milieu therapy. In facilities that utilized individual counseling, the inmate staff ratio was 14.5 to 1. Thus, differences in treatment intervention orientations probably hinge more on treatment philosophy and program "fit" rather than on treatment staff levels.

Just as there was a variety in the treatment modalities offered, a vast array of specific theoretical approaches to substance abuse treatment also were revealed in the findings. As displayed in Table 5.6, of the 22 types of

Section III

INTENSIVE SUPERVISION

Section III is devoted to the intermediate sanction known as intensive probation supervision. IPS programs offer a challenging model to supplement the more routine probation services that are typically offered today. Supervision has always been an integral component of probation services. From the earliest days over a century ago, probation officers have been expected to supervise their charges as well as provide services to the court including the presentence investigation. There has always been a strain on probation departments given the legal requirements regarding presentence investigations. As court dockets and probation caseloads have become overburdened, probation officers have found it harder to devote significant energies to the supervision aspect of their job. They have been forced to opt for "paper probation" in many cases where there is no regular contact with probationers and in most other cases, they have been able to spend less time meeting with probationers because of the size of caseloads.

Partly as a result of increased caseloads and decreased levels of supervision, probation has been intensely scrutinized and often criticized in recent years. Intensive probation supervision programs have been one of the positive responses that probation departments have developed in response to concerns about inadequate supervision. In IPS programs, probation officers generally have caseloads that are small enough to allow for a greater number of contact and lengthier meetings with probationers. Although the smaller caseloads do increase the overall costs of probation, there can nevertheless accrue financial savings as IPS programs are still much less expensive than prison and jail sentences. If IPS programs are found to be effective in preventing further crime and delinquency, then the savings are even more significant as fewer offenders end up being reconvicted and sentenced again.

The papers in this section present a wealth of information regarding the nature, operation, and evaluation of intensive probation supervision programs. The IPS programs discussed in the following pages provide excellent examples of how IPS programs have evolved in recent years and what contributions can be made by these kinds of programs to the overall system of criminal sanctions. It is interesting to note that IPS programs have, in a sense, revived one of the most basic historical probation principles. Since the days of John

Augustus, the most ideal conception of probation has been one that emphasized a close working relationship between the probation officer and the probationer. For well over a century now, the most basic appeal of probation has been that it could allow the offender a chance to avoid further problems with the law by creating a special relationship with the probation officer. There has been much criticism of probation for not yet having met these lofty expectations. However, it is fair to say that probation has not truly been given the opportunity to demonstrate its full potential because of caseload size. Even before the caseload increases of the last decade, probation officers were rarely afforded the "luxury" of caseloads that were really small enough to permit them to explore the full potential of probation services. This is precisely why the IPS programs are such an important development. For the first time on a widespread basis, probation departments are capable of lowering the size of caseloads through IPS to the point where the full potential of probation may be realized. This is an exciting development in the field of corrections.

6

Achieving Public Safety Through Rehabilitation and Reintegration: The Promise of a New ISP

Susan Stone
American Probation and Parole Association

Betsy Fulton
American Probation and Parole Association

INTRODUCTION

There appear to be two conditions that drive program development in corrections: crises and political pressures. The confusion and ambiguities associated with these conditions directly affect program development. The programs that emerge are often designed to meet short-term objectives and immediate needs, rather than to provide long-term solutions. Until community corrections begins to develop and implement programs based on principles of effective correctional intervention, rather than in response to outside forces, program evaluations will continue to yield negative results.

This is particularly true for Intensive Supervision Programs (ISPs) in probation and parole. The evolution of ISPs has come full circle. In the past several decades we have moved from offender-oriented programs in which rehabilitation was the primary emphasis, and enforcement of conditions was secondary, to societally oriented programs grounded in punishment and incapacitation as a means to protect society (Cochran, Corbett & Byrne, 1986; Lipchitz, 1986; O'Leary, 1987; Byrne, 1989; Benekos, 1990). ISPs have changed with the prevailing societal norms, rather than because of lessons learned through the systematic evaluation of practices. Accordingly, today's ISPs are yielding no better results than earlier efforts.

The results of recent research on ISPs are discouraging. Most notably, research conducted by the RAND Corporation indicates that:

- ISPs failed to alleviate prison crowding;
- there were no significant differences between the recidivism rates of ISP offenders and offenders under routine supervision; and
- ISPs cost more than originally thought.

Other research corroborates these results (Byrne & Kelly, 1990; GAO, 1993). Hence, it would appear that the very goals that served as an impetus for the development of ISPs have not been achieved.

At best, what ISPs provide is in-program crime control and an intermediate punishment (GAO, 1993; Tonry, 1990; Harland & Rosen, 1987). In an attempt to gain legislative support and public acceptance for these programs, the current public relations strategies are to emphasize punishment, deterrence, and incapacitation. Program designers have attempted to establish "prison-like controls" over offenders within the community. ISP personnel are directed to increase the level of supervision and to respond quickly to violations. It should not come as any surprise that both the number of contacts and the number of technical violations have increased (Baird & Wagner, 1990; Petersilia & Turner, 1993). If these results are acceptable to the public and to local policymakers, then perhaps ISPs should maintain the status quo. If, however, what these stakeholders truly want is a safer community, ISPs must adopt a new way of doing business.

It is the responsibility of correctional practitioners, researchers, and policymakers to continue the process of discovering the nexus between correctional practices and recidivism reduction. While a lofty aspiration, recidivism reduction translates into public safety, the very reason for the existence of probation and parole. Given the aforementioned findings, where then can ISPs find hope for impacting recidivism and increasing public safety?

Recent research on correctional interventions has found that participation in rehabilitative programming does reduce recidivism (Gendreau & Ross, 1987; Gendreau and Andrews, 1990; Andrews, Bonta & Hoge, 1990). ISP-specific research also suggests a possible relationship between rehabilitative programming and recidivism reduction (Byrne & Kelly, 1990; Jolin & Stipak, 1992; Petersilia & Turner, 1990). This combined body of research provides a powerful agenda for correctional programming and hope for promoting the long-term behavioral change that leads to enhanced community protection.

The authors of this chapter recommend that rather than abandoning ISPs altogether, or continuing with ineffective practices, that current models of ISP be modified to incorporate this available knowledge on effective correctional intervention. What is suggested is that ISPs remain intact but that they change the *way* in which they are intensive by shifting their emphasis from exclusive offenders may be a *more* meaningful form of crime control. Focusing on limited and relevant conditions of probation and parole such as employment, involvement in an educational program, or substance abuse treatment does not mean that offenders will be watched less closely (Petersilia, Peterson & Turner, 1992). It just means that *surveillance* will be conducted through more constructive activities rather than mere contacts as outlined in most ISP supervision standards.

Exercise a Balanced Approach

The third principle of the proposed conceptual framework is a balanced approach to the supervision of offenders. Although a focus and emphasis on treatment and services is advocated, ISPs must provide the full range of probation and parole activities which are designed to meet the objectives of risk-control and reform. Harland and Rosen's (1987:39) reference to medical and mental health analogies explicates the need for a balanced approach: "The discovery and application of drugs that can help control (treat) epilepsy and schizophrenia are not taken as grounds in the helping professions for abandoning simultaneous efforts to experiment with approaches that might produce a more enduring solution (cure)." While the long-term goals of ISPs include long-term behavioral change, the importance of treating and controlling the symptoms is not forgotten. By encompassing a balanced approach, ISPs can achieve both short- and long-term goals.

Maloney, Romig, and Armstrong (1988) discuss three objectives of the juvenile justice system that are easily transferrable to the adult system:

- *accountability* refers to measures taken to ensure that offenders are held responsible for the damages, injury, or loss incurred because of their actions;
- *competency development* refers to providing the offender with the skills and knowledge needed to become a productive and responsible citizen; and
- *community protection* acknowledges that equal emphasis must be placed on ensuring public safety.

These same concepts are generally categorized as intervention, surveillance, and enforcement within the adult probation and parole system.

Intervention includes the entire gamut of treatment and services provided to offenders. As seen previously, the provision of treatment and services is a sound means of control and behavioral reform. Intervention activities play a dual role assisting in both competency development and community protection. Intervention tools could include:

- drug/alcohol treatment programs;
- job skills training;
- mental health counseling; or
- GED classes.

Surveillance involves those activities that relate to monitoring offender activity as well as the social environment of the offender. Monitoring the social surroundings, while extremely important, is often overlooked in the design and development of ISPs. While surveillance activities are directly aimed at community protection, they can take place within those activities labeled as interventions. Surveillance tools could include:

- home visits;
- contact with employers;
- community service; or
- neighborhood contacts.

The enforcement component speaks to the need to hold offenders strictly accountable for their actions. To meet this need there must be a wide range of responses, including custody. Enforcement options could include:

- community service requirements;
- restitution;
- in-patient treatment;
- curfew, house arrest, or electronic monitoring; or
- custody in a halfway house.

Intervention, surveillance, and enforcement are the theoretical constructs within which probation and parole can address the public's concern for feeling safe from conditionally released offenders. A firm, fair, and accountable approach to ISPs can provide short-term control of offenders and long-term behavioral reform.

Bazemore (1992:67) discusses the failure of agencies to operationalize the balanced approach despite the claim that they have adopted the theory or concept. He states that "advocates must clarify what outcomes are in fact intended by the three objectives, how these outcomes are to be measured, and what activities are most likely to get us there." For example, the focus should not be on intervention *activities* (e.g., the number of substance abuse treatment sessions attended, the number of potential employers contacted) but on visible results (e.g., a reduction in drug use as measured by drug tests or days most appropriate for ISP. Another benefit concerns the alleviation of some of the pressure to develop "prison-like" controls within the community. A current public relations strategy used to support the development of diversion ISPs is to assure the public that those prisoners who are being diverted into ISP will be subject to the same tight controls of prison. By targeting offenders already on community supervision, more meaningful types of control and surveillance can be justified. Officers can spend their time and agency resources on supervision activities that address offenders' risk factors such as participation in an employment assistance program or a drug/alcohol treatment program, rather than on maintaining electronic monitoring systems or perfunctory daily contacts.

ELEMENTS OF THE MODEL ISP

The elements of the model ISP to be discussed within this section translate the mission and conceptual framework into concrete organizational and supervision strategies. These elements are regarded as critical to the success of ISPs as they offer the best possible means of managing high-risk/high-need offenders within the community. The elements are directed at rehabilitative and reintegrative purposes with increased public safety being the ultimate goal.

Objectives-Based Management (OBM)

Objectives-based management as developed by Clear and O'Leary (1983) is the managerial system can best serve ISPs, offenders, and the community. The high-risk/high-need target population of the model ISP requires a management system that will keep the organization focused on its purpose—the rehabilitation of high-risk offenders in order to achieve public safety. Objectives-based management (OBM) is just such a system. It focuses every aspect of the organization on its intended purpose by providing continual organizational feedback, evaluation, and planning. Centering management on activities rather than results, allows ISP to lose sight of its ultimate goals and fail to adequately serve its population; this puts the community, offenders, and the organization at risk.

OBM is both a top-down and bottom-up proposition. From upper management, it requires the articulation of the organization's purpose which then informs the decisions made at each level of the organization. From the line staff, the objectives developed for individual offenders as part of the objectives-based case plan support the organization's reason for existing.

The objectives-based case plan provides concrete, attainable milestones for the offender and guides the supervision process towards the goals and purpose of the organization. By focusing on results rather than means, the supervision process is guided towards those results. In an objectives-based management system, the line supervisor is responsible for interpreting organizational aims to line officers' caseload decisions, improving quality control, and making unit resource allocation decisions. Utilizing an OBM system provides the agency administrator with a clear picture of ISP's operations from the line level on up through the organization. This information can be used by the administrator to plan for ISP's needs based on its strengths and weaknesses as identified through aggregated caseload information. Information can also be used for program evaluation purposes, the results of which provide continual feedback to ISP on its operations. ISP's successes and needs can then be communicated internally and externally.

Program evaluation in corrections has been a difficult and haphazardly performed task. Yet, it is critical to ISP's continued viability. OBM provides the tools whereby program evaluation can be performed continually and systematically.

ISP Officers as Facilitators and Advocates

The proposed shift in focus requires that ISP officers act as facilitators and advocates. In addition to performing surveillance-type duties, their role is to see that offenders receive the services they need. "Advocacy is still a necessary and viable model for community corrections. The offender needs an advocate in the community as long as there are barriers to rehabilitation and reintegration. Probation and parole officers need to be advocates for their clients' equal access to housing, jobs, social services, and treatment programs" (Lawrence, 1991:457). This is a difficult role to assume, especially given the dearth of quality treatment resources available to probation departments (Erwin, 1990; Byrne & Kelly, 1989). However, this situation makes the advocacy role of probation officers even more crucial.

Along with acting as facilitators and advocates it is important for officers to establish good interpersonal relationships with offenders. According to Braswell (1989:51), "more than any specific systemic approach to treating offenders, it seems rather the quality and credibility of relationships offenders have with treatment staff and significant others may well have the greater correctional influence." These relationships strengthen informal restraints and therefore may result in increased community control (Byrne, 1990). This shift in emphasis, from the frequency of interaction to the quality of interaction clearly fits within the proposed conceptual framework by promoting long-term behavioral change and by providing a method of informal control.

Small Caseloads

Caseload size has been an ongoing area of discussion. A report from the American Probation and Parole Association's Issues Committee (1991) indicates that the diversity and pluralistic nature of the probation and parole field makes it difficult to state a standard caseload size that can be applied uniformly to all probation and parole agencies. The report states that agencies should base their caseload sizes on:

- their basis for classification (risk, needs, offense);
- contact standards (type and frequency);
- hours of work, leave policies; and
- collateral duties.

Demographic factors should also be considered when determining caseload size. Population density and the size of the geographical area in which services are provided also affect the nature of supervision. For example, whether it is an urban or a rural setting will affect the extent of contact due to the required travel.

In addition to these variances, the differential supervision required for individual offenders (a key strategy in effective supervision) makes it difficult to establish a standard caseload size. The workload concept (i.e., assigning the amount of time required to complete specific tasks, including case supervision) accounts for differential supervision and provides a more accurate and fair description of officer caseloads (APPA Issues Committee, 1991). While there will still be varying levels of supervision required among ISP participants, the fact that they will all be high-risk/high-need will help to narrow the range. A New York State survey (Thibault & Maceri, 1986), accounting for jurisdictional variances across the state, found that the supervision of intensive cases ranged from 3.0 to 4.5 hours, with 116 work hours available during each work month. The 116 hours represents the time available after subtracting civil service leave and holidays, travel, staff and professional meetings, form preparation, and court hearings. Using New York State as an example, these numbers translate to caseload sizes ranging from 20 to 38 cases.

In the past, ISPs have been surveillance and activities-oriented. The new generation of ISPs proposed within this chapter focuses on interventions supported by surveillance and enforcement strategies, is results-oriented rather than activities-oriented, and is working with a higher risk/need population. Common sense indicates that to implement this type of program, time becomes even more of an issue; one that necessitates small caseloads. It is recommended that ISP caseloads range from 20 to 30 offenders per officer depending on the jurisdictional factors outlined above.

The literature clearly indicates that small caseloads alone do not mean better supervision (Banks, Porter, Rardin, Sider & Unger, 1976; Neithercutt & Gottfredson, 1974; Carter & Wilkins, 1976). There is no "magic number" that provides for optimum supervision. Other factors including officer skills and quality of supervision must be combined with small caseloads to achieve effective supervision.

System of Rewards

One principle of effective intervention, as identified by Gendreau and Andrews (1990), is the use of positive reinforcement. However, while most ISPs have an available range of sanctions, few have a system of rewards or emphasize the use of positive reinforcement. For years, institutions have used a system of rewards; those inmates who comply with institutional rules are granted additional privileges and receive time off their sentence (Bartollas, 1985). This concept of reinforcing positive behavior has not been adopted so readily within probation and parole settings. The administrators of a unique program in Bucks County, Pennsylvania, in which offenders can earn "good time" off the length of the program for good behavior, state "the negative consequences are easy to build into a program, but it is the positive consequences which allow for a client to internalize the structure imposed by ISP" (Kelsey, 1991:5). This type of thinking supports the behavior modification theory that assumes that the desired behavior will increase if it is rewarded immediately and systematically (Bartollas, 1985).

Rewards for good behavior and progress on ISP may include the lifting or alleviating of sanctions such as electronic monitoring, house arrest, or curfew; or the honoring of special requests such as for vacations or travel permits. Token systems and behavioral contracts are effective positive reinforcement strategies (Bartollas, 1985). A reward can be something as simple as attention and praise from the probation or parole officer. Gendreau (1993) has stated that the ratio of four rewards to one punitive measure is essential for positive behavioral change. This requires creativity on the part of the probation or parole officer.

System of Sanctions

Agencies need to clearly define technical violations and new arrests, and the appropriate responses to both. Half of the current prison sentences [in California] involve no new crime, but rather violations of conditions (Vasconcellos, 1991 as cited in Scheff, 1992). Instead of incarceration, a more effective response to these technical violations might be to impose a sanction from the next level of surveillance and constraint (Scheff, 1992). Pearson and Harper (1990:84) note the importance of "providing visible progressive sanctions." Sanctions may include, but are not limited to: increased surveillance contacts, community service, curfew, house arrest, electronic monitoring, inpatient treatment, short-term detention, or revocation and incarceration.

Each violation should be followed by the swift imposition of an appropriate sanction, not in the context of punishment but as a means of controlling the offender in the community and holding him/her accountable. The process of imposing sanctions may be by administrative hearing or formal court proceedings. A progressive program gives the probation/parole officer the discre-

7

The Diversionary Effectiveness of Intensive Supervision and Community Corrections Programs*

John T. Whitehead
East Tennessee State University

Larry S. Miller
East Tennessee State University

Laura B. Myers
Sam Houston State University

INTRODUCTION

The State of Tennessee Department of Correction offers two programs—Intensive Probation Supervision and Community Corrections—which are intended to divert jail- and prison-bound felons from incarceration to supervision in the community. Intensive Probation Supervision involves Department of Correction probation officers supervising offenders. Community Corrections involves the contracting out of offenders to private agencies whose personnel provide various types of supervision such as house arrest. Both programs represent intermediate sanctions intended to divert offenders from incarceration.

*The project staff thank the Department of Correction for the opportunity to conduct this research. We are particularly grateful to Susan Mattson for her diligent work in training and supervising the data collection team and for her assistance throughout the project.

RESEARCH PROBLEM

Given the contradictory findings on prior diversion projects, the research problem was to generate an estimation of the degree to which the two Tennessee programs were indeed being used for offenders whom judges normally would sentence to jail or prison if the programs were not in existence. Conversely, the research assessed the degree to which the new programs were being used for offenders who normally would be sentenced to regular probation. The research drew representative samples of felons sentenced to regular probation, intensive probation, community corrections, jail, and prison with probation eligible sentences. The respective samples were analyzed and compared to determine if the intensive probation and community corrections offenders bore closer resemblance to the incarceration samples or to the regular probation sample. Closer similarity to the incarceration samples would suggest that the programs were truly diverting offenders who normally would be incarcerated. Closer resemblance to the regular probation sample would imply that net widening instead of true diversion was occurring. It was anticipated that both processes have been occurring and thus the analysis estimated the proportion of offenders being diverted compared to the proportion not being diverted. Tabular analysis, chi-square statistics, analysis of variance, and discriminant analysis were used to determine measures of the degree of similarity among programs and diversionary estimates. The discriminant analysis results are presented here.

RESEARCH LITERATURE

The Tennessee intensive supervision program and community corrections program are both part of a recent national trend to attempt to relieve prison overcrowding[1] (Greenfeld, 1990) by initiating new programs of intermediate sanctions. These programs of intensive supervision, home confinement, and electronic surveillance are meant to fill the gap between the harsh sanction of prison and the lenient sanction of ordinary probation (McCarthy, 1987; Morris & Tonry, 1990).

Evaluation of these programs is relatively new, but there is controversy whether such programs do actually divert would-be inmates from incarceration or instead capture would-be regular probationers into a more restrictive form of community supervision. Detailed analyses of intensive supervision programs in Florida, Georgia, Kansas, and New Jersey, for example, have indicated that diversion occurred (Baird & Wagner, 1990; Erwin, 1987; Jones, 1990; National Council on Crime and Delinquency, 1990; Pearson & Harper, 1990). Critics, however, have questioned these claims (Byrne, 1990; Byrne, Lurigio & Baird, 1989; Tonry, 1990) and have asserted that many of the new programs have become more punitive options for offenders whom judges would normally *not* incarcerate. The critics contend that net widening often takes place: judges continue to send similar or increased proportions of offenders to incarceration and begin to place persons they would normally place on regular probation into the new so-called "intensive" programs.

One of the most frequently used methods of analyzing the diversionary impact of community sanctions is discriminant analysis. Discriminant analysis has been used in studies of the diversionary impact of community sanctions in the Florida (Baird & Wagner, 1990; National Council on Crime and Delinquency, 1990) and Kansas (Jones, 1990). In Florida, discriminant analysis revealed that 65 percent of the cases were classified correctly; in Kansas, 55 percent were classified correctly. It should be noted that Florida uses sentencing guidelines that may contribute to the greater accuracy of discriminant analysis in that state. In both Florida and Kansas, legal variables such as prior record and offense severity and social variables such as education and history of drug abuse were used to predict sentence type.

Perhaps the best summary of prior research is the conclusion that programs divert some percentage of the offenders they supervise away from prison. For example, sophisticated analyses of the precise levels of diversionary impact in Florida and Georgia indicated that slightly more than half of the offenders in those programs were indeed diverted from incarceration (Baird & Wagner, 1990; Erwin, 1987). Similarly, a study in Kansas found that "community corrections programs in the two largest participating counties did have a significant impact on prison admissions of program-eligible offenders" but that "[T]his is not to say that net-widening did not occur" (Jones, 1990:96-97).

Additionally, it is interesting to note that the one program that used a research design capable of a clear demonstration of whether diversion was taking place did not even claim to be diverting offenders away from prison. California's intensive supervision programs, which are actually probation enhancement programs, have utilized an experimental design with random assignment of offenders. Rather than attempt to divert offenders from prison, California officials have "selected persons currently on probation whom they judged in need of more intensive supervision—participants were either high risk when granted probation or were showing signs of failing and potential revocation" (Petersilia & Turner, 1990:95). Ironically, this decision to divert from probation rather than from prison resulted in California's programs having offenders at higher risk levels than Georgia's intensive program, which was supposed to be diverting people from prison. Unfortunately, hoped-for recidivism reductions did not result (Petersilia & Turner, 1991).

These findings on the debate over the ability of the new intensive supervision programs to divert offenders from prison would be surprising except for the fact that they are new examples of old truths rather than totally new

discoveries. Prior research on programs intended to divert juveniles from official court processing has often found that juvenile courts continued to process
consistent proportions of youths and simply expanded their reach to include
juveniles who would have been ignored prior to the existence of the new programs (Lundman, 1993). Similarly, much of the research on community alternatives prior to recent developments in intensive supervision, electronic
monitioring, and house arrest indicated that often those alternatives were not
diverting offenders from incarceration (Austin & Krisberg, 1982; Hylton,
1982). Thus, findings that new generation community correctional programs
are not diverting all of their charges from prison should not surprise anyone
familiar with the history of criminal justice.

METHODOLOGY

Hypotheses

This review of the literature suggests that Tennessee's two new programs
are probably diverting some but not all of their caseloads from prison and are
drawing some proportion of their subjects from the pool of offenders who
would normally be placed on regular probation. More specifically, two
hypotheses appear plausible:

1.   Some percentage (studies in Florida and Georgia suggest slightly
     over 50 percent) of the offenders placed on intensive supervision
     and community corrections supervision resemble inmates who
     were probation eligible at the time of their sentencing more
     closely than regular probationers. Conversely, a certain percent-
     age more closely resemble regular probationers than inmates
     who were probation eligible at sentencing.

2.   The implementation of intensive probation supervision and com-
     munity corrections has had some impact on decreasing prison
     and jail populations in Tennessee.

Data and Methods

Since Tennessee has not been using an experimental design with random
assignment of eligible offenders into the various correctional options, it was
only possible to examine the question of the degree to which the programs
have been diverting offenders from jail or prison in an indirect manner. The
strategy we used was to compare and contrast samples of offenders from
intensive probation and community corrections with offenders in prison and in
jail and on regular probation. Given the diversionary intent of the Tennessee

programs, intensive supervision and community corrections offenders should most nearly resemble incarcerated offenders rather than regular probationers.

To develop a profile of intensive supervision probationers and community corrections offenders compared to prison and jail inmates on the one hand and regular probationers on the other hand, we attempted to draw random samples of 350 felony offenders in each category for a total combined sample of approximately 1,750 offenders. A sample this size would minimize sampling error, allow for the possibility of missing data, and allow for various subgroup analyses. Although this would have been the ideal sampling procedure, practical concerns made it necessary to employ some modifications. In consultation with the Department of Correction, a simple random proportionate to size sample was agreed upon initially. This meant that within the designated time frame (offenders sentenced between 1989 and 1991) the samples of the five populations would reflect their actual proportion in the population. The samples would also reflect proportions by county. The Department of Correction however, faced data collection problems in some areas. Unreliable case files, especially on prisoners and jailees, led the Department to modify the proportions somewhat. For example, in Shelby County (Memphis), incarcerees actually constituted 43 percent of the sentenced population but the percentage of the sample offenders who had been sentenced to incarceration was 35 percent. In the Nashville area, incarcerees actually constituted 16 percent of the offender population, but 47 percent of our sample offenders from that area were incarcerees. These deviations from the original sampling plan should be kept in mind when interpreting findings about the incarcerees.

Information on each offender's offense, prior record, demographic characteristics (age, sex, race, etc.), and social characteristics (employment status at the time of the offense, drug and alcohol problems, health, etc.) was compiled from Department of Correction central office records/computer databases and/or from individual offender folders/pre-sentence/post-sentence records at the appropriate local unit. This information was then coded and entered onto a computer readable data file. The Department of Correction collected the data. The authors assisted in monitoring the data collection process to a limited extent to insure proper sampling and data collection. The authors and several graduate assistants then coded the data and supervised the data entry process. Our data analysis involved bivariate analyses and a discriminant analysis, but only the discriminant analysis findings are presented here.

FINDINGS

In most of the analyses that follow, offender category was collapsed into three groups: (1) regular probationers; (2) intermediate sanction offenders (intensive probationers and community corrections offenders); and, (3) incarcerees (prisoners and jailees). Logic and empirical considerations justified collapsing the five offender categories into these three groups. Logically, intensive probation and community corrections both represent intermediate sanctions harsher than regular probation but not as harsh as the deprivation of liberty which incarceration represents. Prison and jail sentences both involve serious deprivation of liberty. As will be shown below, discriminant analysis of the data correctly classified a much higher percentage of the cases into three groups rather than five groups.

Characteristics of the Sample

Sample members were mostly white males with an average age of about 28. Many of the offenders had alcohol or drug problems. Over one-half had prior arrests. There were several notable differences in the three groups of the 1,458 offenders in the sample. For example, only 35 percent of the regular probationers were not employed at the time of the offense compared to over 50 percent in the other two sentence categories. Over one-half of the incarceration sample was nonwhite. The regular probation category had the lowest percentage of persons with an alcohol problem and the lowest percentage of persons who used drugs during the two years prior to the offense. The intermediate sanction offenders and the incarcerees both had higher proportions of offenders with juvenile conviction and incarceration histories. Both the number of prior arrests and the offense severity rankings (a lower ranking represents a more serious offense) increased across the three sentence types.

Discriminant Analysis Findings

Discriminant analysis[2] was used to determine what, if any, groups of offenders existed in the sample based on legal and social variables associated with sentencing in previous theoretical and empirical studies. In other words, we knew that judges across the state had sentenced or classified the sample into five categories ranging from regular probation to prison. We were now asking the computer to classify these same offenders based on such independent variables as seriousness of the offense, prior record, custody status at time of sentencing, race, employment status and so forth. A complete list of the 14 independent variables, along with the coding scheme used in the analysis, is displayed in Table 7.1.[3]

When the number of groups was set at five (to correspond with the actual groups in the sample), discriminant analysis was able to classify correctly 40 percent of the cases.[4] For example, discriminant analysis correctly identified 129 of the 247 offenders the judges actually put on probation and 31 of the 72 offenders the judges actually put into prison.

We then set the number of groups at three by collapsing the intensive probationers and the community corrections offenders into one group and the prisoners and jailees into one group. As noted above, we combined these offenders on the logical argument that intensive probation and community corrections are both more intensive forms of community control (both represent intermediate sanctions) and that prison and jail both represent incarceration or radical deprivation of liberty.

Table 7.1
Variables and Coding Schemes for the Discriminant Analysis

Custody status: 0=bond, ROR, or pre-trial release; 1=in custody
Previous arrests: actual number of prior arrests
Previous felony arrests: actual number of prior felony arrests
Offense seriousness: offense severity rank used by Tennessee
    Department of Corrections*
Drug offense: 0=non-drug offense; 1=drug offense
Defense attorney: 0=private; 1=appointed, public defender, or other
Number of pending charges: actual number of pending charges at sentencing
Number of unique felony convictions: actual number of felony convictions
Adjudication status: 0=pled guilty or no contest; 1=found guilty at trial
Victim: 0=no victim; 1=victim
Employment status: 0=not employed at time of offense; 1=employed
    (verified employment, claimed self-employment, or in military) at
    time of offense
Drug problem: 0=no drug abuse problem at time of offense; 1=offender had
    a drug abuse problem at time of offense
Gender: 0=female; 1=male
Race:0=white; 1=all others

*A Department of Correction staff attorney, who had worked with the Sentencing Commission in developing the 1989 revised criminal code assigned ranks within the felony classes (A, B, C, D, E) giving priority to crimes against persons, followed by drug offenses, then crimes against property. It is not a true interval scale in that each point may not reflect the same difference in degree of severity, but it is continuous and reflects overall seriousness of offense.

As Table 7.2 indicates, using three groups, discriminant analysis was able to classify correctly over one-half of the offenders (52.6%). The analysis correctly identified two-thirds (65.9%) of the offenders whom the judges placed on regular probation, 194 (42.2%) of the 460 offenders placed into intensive or community corrections, and 104 of the 171 (60.8%) of the incarcerees.

As Table 7.3 indicates, both discriminant functions in this model[5] were significant, with the first accounting for 72 percent of the total between-groups variability. The total variability explained by the differences between groups is approximately 25 percent[6] (26.8% to be exact), suggesting that the three sentence groups—regular probation, intermediate sanction (intensive probation-community corrections), incarceration—are not easily distinguishable.

Table 7.2
Classification Results Using Three Groups (Row %s)

Actual Group		Predicted Group Membership		
	N	1	2	3
1. Regular Probation	255	66%	18%	16%
		168	47	40
2. Intermediate Sanction	460	30%	42%	27%
		140	194	126
3. Incarceration	171	23%	16%	61%
		40	27	104
Column Totals:	886	348	268	270

Percent of "grouped" cases correctly classified: 52.6%
886 cases had no missing discriminating variables.

Table 7.3
Canonical Discriminant Functions

Function	Eigenvalue	Percent of Variance	Canonical Correlation
1	.23	72	.43
2	.09	28	.29

After Function	Wilks' Lambda	Chi²	D.F.	Significance
0	.75	245.33	24	.0000
1	.92	71.785	11	.0000

In short, discriminant analysis was able to predict a substantial proportion of the sentences. The discriminant analysis, however, also showed some differences between its predictions and actual sentences. We will explain this using the discriminant analysis with three groups. The statistical technique of discriminant analysis predicted that 67 of the 171 offenders who were incarcerated fit into either the regular probation or the intensive probation-community corrections category. Based on the legal and social variables available to the computer, it saw these 67 individuals as most resembling non-incarcerees rather than incarcerees. On the other hand, the computer program predicted that 126 of the 460 offenders who actually received intensive probation-community corrections and 40 of the 255 offenders who received regular probation actually resembled the incarcerees. Finally, 140 of the offenders who were predicted to fit into the regular probation category actually were sentenced to intensive probation or community corrections.

There are at least two ways to interpret these findings. One interpretation is that the discriminant analysis suggests that some offenders are being sentenced too harshly—they are getting an incarcerative sentence when they resemble offenders who do *not* get incarcerated or they are getting an intensive probation-community corrections sanction even though they most resemble persons on regular probation. The analysis also suggests that some offenders are being treated too leniently—they resemble incarcerees but actually get a non-incarcerative sentence or they resemble the middle intensive probation-community corrections category but actually are sentenced to regular probation. In other words, actual sentences represent some diversion and some net widening. The offenders for whom the discriminant analysis predicted incarceration but who actually stayed in the community can be considered to be diverted from prison. The offenders whom the statistical tool predicted to fit into regular probation but received intensive probation or community corrections represent net widening.

Table 7.4
Summary Table: Statistically Significant Discriminating Variables in the Final Model

Step #	Variable	Wilks' Lambda	Variable Label
1	CUSTSTAT	.89	Custody status at sentencing
2	DRUGPROB	.86	Presence of drug problem
3	PREFELAR	.83	# of prior felony arrests
4	DEFATTY	.81	Type of defense attorney
5	CONRANK	.79	Conviction offense severity ranking
6	DRUGS	.78	Drug offense
7	OFFEMPL	.77	Offender's employment status
8	PREARR	.76	# of prior adult arrests
9	UNIQFELC	.76	# of unique felony convictions
10	PENDING	.75	# of pending charges at sentencing
11	GENDER	.75	Offender's gender
12	RACE	.75	Offender's race

Note: Adjudication status and victim did *not* enter the equation.

It is also instructive to examine the variables which the discriminant analysis revealed to be significant correlates of sentence type. Table 7.4 shows the 12 significant discriminating variables in the stepwise order they entered the analysis and the respective Wilks' lambda statistic for each. Several of these variables merit special attention. Custody status was the first variable to enter the analysis. Its importance suggests that judges are making an early determination of sentence. The legal variables of prior felony arrests, conviction offense severity ranking, and prior adult arrests were correlates of the sentencing. As expected, judges do consider both the seriousness of the offense and the prior record of the offender. Whether the offense was a drug offense compared to all other types of offenses was also one of the significant discriminating variables. The importance of gender and race suggests that sentencing decisions reflect these two nonlegal factors to some extent: males and nonwhites are more likely to be incarcerated than females and whites. The offender's employment status at the time of the offense and whether the offender had a drug problem also influence the sentencing decision.

Additional discriminant analyses showed that the inclusion of only a few variables could produce a more parsimonious model. The inclusion of just four discriminating variables—custody status, number of prior arrests, offense severity, and sex, for example, resulted in 44 percent of the three groups being correctly classified. When race was added to these four variables, 45 percent of the three groups were correctly classified.

It should be noted that several discriminant analyses were run with the so-called Greenwood scale and with selected variables used to calculate the Greenwood scale.[7] Although both the entire scale and its individual variables proved to be significant predictors of sentence type, the high number of missing values associated with the scale in this data set dictated that it not be used in the final models.

Given departmental experience and expectation that region might be an important correlate of sentence type, we ran some additional analyses to examine the impact of region. We did separate analyses for the Delta region, the Mid-Cumberland region, the rest of the state except the Delta and Mid-Cumberland regions, and the entire state excluding the Delta region. Those discriminant analyses indicated that the Delta region had greater classification accuracy than the other regions. Using three groups, the Delta region discriminant analysis correctly classified 69 percent of the cases, the mid-Cumberland region 54 percent, and all other regions (excluding Delta and mid-Cumberland) combined 51 percent. If we included the mid-Cumberland region with all the others except Delta, the accuracy was 49 percent. The significant variables in the Delta region were a drug problem, defense attorney, unique felony convictions, custody status, offender employment status, number of pending charges, prior arrests, prior felony arrests, and offense severity ranking. The significant variables in the analysis for all the regions except Delta were the following: custody status, number of prior felony arrests, offense severity ranking, a drug problem, offender employment status, number of prior arrests, race, drug offense versus all other types of offense, gender, number of pending charges, unique felony convictions, defense attorney, and victim. It is interesting that race was not a factor in the Delta region. Also, whether the offender had a drug problem was a factor in both the Delta region and all other regions combined, but whether the offense was a drug offense was not a factor in the Delta region.

DISCUSSION

The major finding of the research is that some diversion and some net widening appear to have taken place. Intensive probation and community corrections are accomplishing their stated objective of diverting some offenders from incarceration but they are also being used for some offenders who normally would be sentenced to regular probation.

The exact extent of diversion from prison and the precise extent of net widening are impossible to determine but can be estimated in several ways. One way to count the number of divertees is to add up the offenders predicted to be in intensive probation or community corrections who actually were sentenced to those dispositions (194) and the number of offenders who were predicted to be in prison but actually were sentenced to intensive probation or community corrections (126) for a total of 320 offenders diverted. The argument could be made that if intensive probation and community corrections did not exist as sentencing options, then judges may have sentenced these offenders to incarceration. Because the discriminant analysis omitted those cases with missing values on the discriminating variables (see Note 3), it is important to translate the estimate of the numbers diverted into a percentage. The 320 offenders whom the discriminant analysis shows to have been diverted represent 69.6 percent of the intermediate sanction offenders and 36.1 percent of the 886 offenders used for the printed output. Thus, the discriminant analysis could be cited to conclude that approximately 70 percent of the offenders in intensive probation or community corrections were diverted from prison. Changing the base from the intermediate sanction offenders to all offenders, a little over one-third of the probation-eligible offenders were indeed diverted. This is the most generous way to estimate the percentage diverted.

The diversion argument is clearly stronger for the 126 offenders that discriminant analysis identified as resembling incarcerees. It is most likely that if the new intermediate sanctions had not existed at the time of sentencing, then judges would have sentenced all or nearly all of these individuals to prison or jail rather than to regular probation. It is less clear what would have happened to the 194 offenders predicted to be sentenced and actually sentenced to an intermediate sanction.

One way to shed some light on this question is to make a conservative assumption that if the intermediate sanctions were not in existence at the time of sentencing, then judges would have sentenced half of these 194 offenders

to incarceration and half to regular probation. Based on this assumption of a
50/50 split, 223 offenders (126 plus 97) would have been incarcerated and
237 offenders (140 plus 97) would have received regular probation.
Translating these numbers to percentages, slightly less than one-half (48.5%)
of the offenders placed on an intermediate sanction would have gone to
prison and slightly more than one-half (51.5%) would have been placed on
regular probation.

    If you use the total sample of probation-eligible offenders as the base for
computing percentages, the estimates in the preceding paragraph convert to
the following: 25.2 percent (223/886)[8] of all the probation-eligible offenders
were diverted from prison to an intermediate sanction and 26.7 percent
(237/886) of the offenders were placed in an intermediate sanction when they
probably would have received regular probation if the intermediate sanction
did not exist.

    After all this, a logical question is whether these findings translate into a
positive or negative judgment about the intensive probation and community
corrections programs in Tennessee? Positively, the programs appear to have
diverted at least 48.5 percent of the intermediate sanction offenders (relying
on the conservative estimate discussed above); arguably, the programs freed
up that amount of prison beds. Critics would hasten to point out that the programs easily widened the net of social control. Most generously, the programs
incarcerated an unnecessay 30 percent; 51.5 percent if one uses the estimate
based on those who would have been placed on regular probation. The answer
to the evaluative question thus depends on a number of factors. It depends on
whether you use generous or conservative estimates of the number of offenders diverted and the number of offenders caught up in net widening. It
depends on cost estimates for the various sanctions. It also depends on other
goals for the program, such as recidivism and public opinion, which go
beyond the objectives of this research project.

IMPLICATIONS

    The clearest finding of this research on the diversionary effectiveness of
intermediate sanctions in Tennessee is that both diversion and net widening
occurred. Some offenders received intensive probation or community corrections who statistically resembled incarcerees and some offenders who were
sentenced to an intermediate sanction statistically resembled regular probationers. A generous estimate is that the new intermediate sanctions diverted
70 percent of the offenders who received an intermediate sanction from incarceration; this represents a diverting of 36 percent of all probation-eligible
offenders. A more conservative estimate is that intensive probation and community corrections only diverted about one-half (48.5%) of the intermediate

sanction offenders from incarceration, which is approximately one-fourth (25%) of all probation-eligible offenders. Conversely, the discriminant analysis suggests that between 30 percent and 51.5 percent of the offenders actually sentenced to an intermediate sanction would have received regular probation had intensive probation and community corrections not existed at the time of their sentencing. Expressed in percentages, the analysis suggests that 16 percent (140/886) to 27 percent (237/886) of all probation-eligible offenders represent net widening.[9]

The research project staff feels that that conservative diversion estimates (48.5% of the intermediate sanction offenders and 25% of all probation-eligible offenders) and corresponding net-widening estimates (51.5% of the intermediate sanction offenders and 27% of all probation-eligible offenders) represent the most plausible estimates of what actually occurred. These figures represent a cautious assumption of what the judges would have done if the new intermediate sanctions had not been in place. We emphasize, however, that this reasoning is based on the discriminant analyses and the assumption discussed above.

These figures suggest that if diversion is the only (or the primary) objective of intensive probation and community corrections, then the efforts of the state may be misguided. A slightly higher percentage of offenders are being caught in a wider net than are being diverted from prison. A cost-benefit analysis could clarify the debate. In other words, dollar estimates of the costs of incarceration and the intermediate sanctions could illustrate the fiscal consequences of our research.

It needs to be emphasized, however, that diversion need not be the only rationale for the use of intermediate sanctions such as intensive probation and community corrections. Intermediate sanctions simply make sense. Numerous writers have pointed out that traditional probation was originally intended for nonserious offenders and that its mission and effectiveness have been diluted by expecting that a sanction originally intended for nonserious offenders could be simply expanded to include more serious offenders. Likewise many writers have decried the unnecessary use of incarceration for less serious offenders and the lack of a set of meaningful intermediate punishments for those offenders too dangerous for probation but not quite deserving of prison. Irrespective of diversion versus net widening considerations, it seems that a multi-layered set of sanctions is more rational than a simple dichotomy (probation-incarceration). As Morris and Tonry put it:

> Effective and principled punishment of convicted criminals requires the development and application of a range of punishments between imprisonment and probation. Imprisonment is used excessively; probation is used even more excessively; between the two is a near-vacuum of purposive and enforced punishments (1990:3).

If the state wishes to improve the consistency of the decisions about sentencing, it seems that several options are available. One option would be to eliminate the intermediate sanctions. A two-group discriminant analysis (not reported above) showed that a basic in-out decision could result in greater classification accuracy. Eliminating intensive probation and community corrections, however, is a drastic solution that also eliminates the positive effects of these relatively new programs. The existence of these programs may mean that offenders in the community are receiving meaningful sanctions rather than the slap on the wrist that regular probation is often accused of representing.

A second option to improve the accuracy of the decisions about sentencing is to influence the judges to be more systematic in assessing those who qualify for incarceration and those who make good candidates for community supervision. One possibility is to enact a more objective and limiting set of sentencing guidelines that judges are bound to follow unless they provide written justification for departing from the guidelines. As noted above, Florida has more restrictive guidelines and an analysis of diversion in that state showed greater ability to correctly classify cases into regular probation, intermediate sanctions, or incarceration (National Council on Crime and Delinquency, 1990). Tennessee reformed its sentencing legislation in 1989,[10] but the new law still leaves a great deal of discretion in the hands of state judges. For example, judges have a three- to six-year sentencing range for a Standard Class C felon and a two- to four-year range for a Standard Class D felon (Tennessee Sentencing Commission, 1990). Thus nonresidential burglary (a Class D felony in Tennessee) can result in a prison sentence of 2 to 4 years in Tennessee (a two-year range) whereas the same offense is a non-prison offense in Minnesota (with a possible jail sentence up to 12 months), merits 2.5 to 18 months incarceration in Pennsylvania, or 3 to 9 months of incarceration in Washington State (Morris & Tonry, 1990:53).

Another option to improve the accuracy of the decisions about sentencing is to improve the presentence investigation process. For example, it might be helpful to provide the judges with the offense seriousness rankings used by the Department of Correction. Those seriousness rankings proved to be one of the significant variables in the discriminant analyses noted in this research. In fact, seriousness rankings also proved to be one of the four variables used in the parsimonious model that used a very limited set of variables to achieve a level of predictive accuracy almost as high as when all 14 final model variables were included in the analyses. Similarly, the Greenwood scale proved to be a significant correlate of sentencing when it was included in the equations. It was not used in the final equations, however, because many of the component items had high numbers of missing values. If probation officers made it a point to ensure that presentence reports included the information ascertained in the Greenwood scale (see Note 7 for a description of those items), the accuracy of the decisions about sentencing would improve.

One of the implications of the research is that presentence reports can be shortened considerably. As noted, 12 variables were statistically significant in the final discriminant analyses and even four or five variables resulted in classifications approximately as accurate as those based on 12 variables. It is possible that a greatly shortened presentence report focusing on prior record, offense seriousness, employment history, substance abuse history, and a few other items would provide enough information for judges. This implication is consistent with prior research on probation officer decisionmaking which found that probation officers use only a few pieces of information to make sentence recommendations (Carter, 1967).

The analysis also suggests that judges may be paying undue attention to some nonlegal considerations. The inclusion of both gender and race in the final model suggests that males and nonwhites are being treated with disparity compared to females and whites. Once again, sentencing guidelines could reduce this tendency, as has occurred in Pennsylvania (Kramer & Lubitz, 1985).

SUMMARY

Intensive probation and community corrections programs in Tennessee appear to be diverting some offenders from incarceration, but they are also being used for many offenders who would normally be sentenced to regular probation. In fact, a higher percentage of offenders are experiencing a net widening effect than are being diverted. Assuming that the state is committed to the new intermediate sanctions and will not eliminate them, it seems that the state should concentrate some effort on improving the selection of offenders for the two intermediate sanctions. It could do this by opting for some sort of sentencing guidelines system that would put limitations on judicial discretion. Another alternative would be to improve the information provided to judges at sentencing. Consideration should be given to providing essential information to judges such as the number of prior adult arrests, the number of prior felony arrests, offense seriousness, employment history, and information pertaining to the Greenwood scale or some similar scale measuring each offender's risk of future offending. If any of these measures were adopted, a new evaluation of the diversionary impact of the intermediate sanctions would be able to determine their impact on improving the results discussed in this research.

Finally, the state should consider the position of Morris and Tonry (1990) that diversion should not be the primary focus of any intermediate sanction efforts and that net widening should not be that troublesome. According to Morris and Tonry (1990) the primary focus should be on establishing a reasoned set of sanctions. Taking that position, any future evaluation of the intermediate sanctions should examine additional questions such as are new sanctions really intermediate steps between regular probation and incarceration? How are new sanctions perceived by judges, corrections personnel, offenders, victims, and the public? Do new sanctions help clarify the mission of probation? And, finally, how do new sanctions affect recidivism? Diversionary impact and net widening are important concerns, but not the only ones. Future evaluation studies need to focus on the multiple goals and consequences of both intensive probation and community corrections.

NOTES

[1]   For example, in December 1989, Tennessee had approximately 8,000 inmates in Department of Correction institutions, a 9.9 percent increase over the 1986 figure (Tennessee Department of Correction, 1990).

[2]   Discriminant analysis attempts to locate some function of the predictor variable scores (a linear combination) which can be used to assign observations with proper scores into the appropriate group (Dillon & Goldstein, 1984). The pupose of multiple dscriminant analysis is to discover linear composites (discriminant axes) of the predictor variables such that the ratio of between-groups to within-groups variability is as large as possible. Each composite must be uncorrelated with all other extracted composites. The analysis is also used to determine which of the predictor variables are contributing the most to the classification of the groups. If this cannot be accomplished, then the predictor variables are not being used as hypothesized for the classification. If the analysis does produce clear discriminations among the groups, then new cases can be assigned correctly to the groups based on an observation's predictor variable profile and resultant scores on the linear composites.

[3]   We tried several sets of discriminating variables before settling on this set of 14. We first entered a lengthy set of legal variables (variables relating to prior record, custody status, type of defense attorney, etc.). We then entered a lengthy set of social variables (age, sex, race, employment status, drug history, etc.). We then used a combined set of legal and social variables. We also examined in considerable detail the Greenwood scale and its component variables (see text). We settled on this set of discriminating variables based on logic and prior research and on the relative success of these variables in correctly classifying cases. That is, both logic and prior research suggest the importance of such variables as prior record, offense severity, employment status, and so forth. Empirically, this set of 14 variables correctly classified higher percentages of cases than other sets we used and/or had fewer missing values than other sets.

[4]   Technically, the analysis correctly identified the percentages noted *for those offenders with no missing values on the discriminating variables in the analysis discussed.*

5   When the dependent variable comprises three groups, two separate discriminant functions are calculated. The null hypothesis is one of no difference among the populations from which the samples are selected, reflecting only sampling variability. The lambda and associated significance values permit the rejection of the null hypothesis for both discriminant functions.

6   Calculated from the square of the canonical correlation for each function.

7   The Greenwood (1984) prediction scale items measure prior conviction for the instant offense, incarceration in the two years preceding the instant offense, conviction as a juvenile, time served in a state juvenile correctional facility, drug use as a juvenile and as an adult, incarceration in the previous two years, and whether employed less than 50 percent of the preceding two years. Unfortunately, many of these items had an excessive number of missing values in the data set.

8   The reader is reminded that these numbers refer to the cases without missing values in the three groups discriminant analysis. The percentages cited needed to be conceptualized for all 1,458 offenders in the sample and for all applicable offenders in the state.

9   It needs to be added that the discriminant analysis also suggests that 87 of the 886 offenders in the analysis were "too tough" for regular probation. These offenders were "predicted" to be either intermediate sanction offenders or incarcerees. Similarly, 67 of the offenders who were incarcerated were "predicted" to have received a lesser sentence. Although our report focuses on the intermediate sanction offenders, the discriminant analysis indicates that misclassifications occur in reference to all three types of sentence.

10 Since the sample contains offenders sentenced under the old sentencing law and the reform law, it is unclear what impact the new law had on the results of the study. Given that the new law is much less limiting than the more specific guidelines in other states (see example in text), it is doubtful that a study of only offenders sentenced under the new law would find very different results.

8

Intensive Supervision
in a Rural County:
Diversion and Outcome*

Stephen Haas
University of Cincinnati

Edward J. Latessa
University of Cincinnati

INTRODUCTION

Faced with an overcrowded prison system, criminal justice professionals and policymakers are being forced to search for alternative ways to sanction criminal offenders. A host of intermediate sanctions designed to treat the criminal offender in the community are being evaluated. These intermediate punishments include boot camps, house arrest, community service, restitution, and intensive supervision. The purpose of these intermediate punishments is to provide correctional alternatives to long-term confinement.

The U.S. Department of Justice (1990:3) defines intermediate sanctioning as "a punishment option that is considered on a continuum to fall between traditional probation and traditional incarceration." Intermediate sanctions were largely developed out of the need to relieve prison crowding and satisfy the general public's desire for new correctional alternatives. Thus, policymakers and researchers began to experiment with programs to punish, control, and reform felons in the community.

---

*The authors would like to thank Beth Sanders and Bruce Gibson for their assistance on this project.

The purpose of this study is to evaluate an intensive supervision program located in Clermont County, Ohio. A sample of intensive and regular probationers were selected and analyzed to determine whether any significant differences existed between the two groups in terms of classification and program outcome. The research focuses on two issues: offender diversion and public safety. In addition, issues are also discussed that are specific to the operation of an IPS in a small rural community. This study is important because it will aid in providing better insight into the effectiveness of IPS as a community-based intermediate sanction.

NEED FOR INTENSIVE SUPERVISION

The major concern facing the American correctional scene today is prison crowding. Despite massive prison construction projects in a number of states, the demand for prison beds has gone largely unabated. Alternatives to confinement have become a necessity rather than an option (American Correctional Association (1990). Rosenthal (1989:1) contends that "the prohibitive costs of constructing and operating jails and prisons make it fiscally impossible to build our way out of the current corrections crises, even if public sentiment continues to favor a 'get tough on crime' posture."

In 1987, construction costs averaged $42,000 per bed and ranged as high as $116,000 per bed; the annual incarceration expense for a single prisoner averages $14,000 but may range as high as $36,500 (Petersilia, 1987). If alternative sanctions are to become reality they must gain public, legislative, and judicial support, and "be perceived as reasonably safe; address the public's desire for punishment through community control, nonpaid labor, and victim restitution; and offer an opportunity for positive change by providing treatment and employment skills" (American Correctional Association, 1990:2).

PREVIOUS INTENSIVE SUPERVISION PROGRAMS

One intermediate, community-based sanction that meets the above criteria is intensive supervision. However, intensive supervision is hardly a new idea. Previous experiments with intensive supervision carried the common goal of maintaining public safety, but differed from the "new generation" of intensive supervision programs in fundamental ways (Latessa, 1986). Earlier versions of intensive supervision were based on the idea that increased client contact would enhance rehabilitation while allowing for greater client control. For example, California's Special Intensive Parole Unit experiments in the 1950s and the San Francisco Project in the 1960s were designed as intensive supervision, but emphasized rehabilitation as the main goal. Later, with rehabilitation as the main objective, experiments were, "undertaken to determine the 'best' caseload size for the community supervision, despite the illogic of the proposition that a magical 'best' number could be found" (Clear, Flynn & Shapiro, 1987:33). The failure of these experiments to produce results fueled two decades worth of cynicism about the general utility of community-based methods. Several authors contend that today's intensive supervision programs emphasize punishment and control of the offender (Burkhart, 1986; Pearson, 1987). However, the rehabilitative aspect of these types of programs has not been forsaken entirely (Clear & Latessa, 1993). Further, current programs are designed to meet the primary goal of easing the burden of prison overcrowding.

DEFINITION OF INTENSIVE SUPERVISION

Today, no two jurisdictions define intensive supervision in the same way. However, one characteristic of all IPS programs is that they provide stricter terms of probation. As Jones (1991:1) points out: "Their common feature is that more control is to be exerted over the offender than that described as probation in that jurisdiction and that often these extra control mechanisms involve restrictions on liberty of movement, coercion into treatment programs, employment obligations, or all three." This increased level of control is usually achieved through reduced caseloads, increased number of contacts, and a range of required activities for participating offenders that can include: victim restitution; community service; employment; random urine and alcohol testing; electronic monitoring; and payment of a probation supervision fee. Offenders may be sentenced to IPS programs by judges, parole boards, or probation agencies. Intensive supervision programs vary in terms of the number and type of contacts per month, caseload size, type of surveillance conducted, and services offered. In addition, programs vary depending upon whether they are staffed by specially trained officers or regular probation officers, and whether an officer 'team' approach is used. In the Spring of 1986, Byrne conducted a survey on the use of intensive supervision across the United States. He found that there was a great deal of variation in the number of personal contacts, ranging from two per month to seven per week. Furthermore, some programs specified curfew checks while others did not. He also found that the ideal caseload size for IPS officers was about 15, yet most officers carried caseloads of approximately 25 offenders (Byrne, 1986).

ISSUES FOR INTENSIVE SUPERVISION

Intensive probation supervision (IPS) as a technique for increasing control over offenders in the community has gained widespread popularity. A 1988 survey found that 45 states had or were developing IPS programs. In 1990, all states, plus the federal system, had some kind of intensive supervision program in place (U.S. Department of Justice, 1990). Widespread acceptance has provided states with the needed continuum of sentencing options. The popularity of intensive supervision has generated a number of policy issues.

Perhaps the most important issue of IPS centers on its effectiveness. Measures of effectiveness vary depending on program goals and objectives. For instance, the goals of a treatment-oriented IPS differ from the goals of a program that places emphasis on offender punishment and control. Notwithstanding the diversity in IPS goals and objectives, Byrne, Lurigio, and Baird (1989:10), have isolated two goals common to most IPS programs. First, "Intensive probation supervision is expected to divert offenders from incarceration in order to alleviate prison overcrowding, avoid the exorbitant costs of building and sustaining prisons, and prevent the stultifying and stigmatizing effects of imprisonment." Secondly, IPS programs are expected to promote public safety through increased surveillance, while promoting a sense of responsibility and accountability through probation fees, restitution, and community service activities.

CLERMONT COUNTY'S INTENSIVE SUPERVISION PROGRAM

Clermont County (population 150,187; Bureau of Census, 1990) is a predominantly white (98.6%), rural county in Southern Ohio. The Clermont County Adult Probation Department established intensive probation in December 1989.[1] The Department operates with a staff of six probation officers. One full-time and one part-time probation officer provide intensive supervision to caseloads of approximately 25 to 30 and 15 to 20 probationers, respectively.

Classification of Offenders

The IPS program in Clermont County accepts only those offenders who are considered too "high-risk" for regular probation: offenders revoked from regular probation, shock probationers, offenders with amended sentences, and offenders who would normally be incarcerated. Offenders who commit offenses of a violent nature, show patterns of habitual violence, or face maximum sentences of less than six months are not eligible for IPS.

Methods of Supervision

The Clermont County Adult Probation Department believes that the first two months of client supervision determine success or failure for most proba-

RESEARCH DESIGN AND SAMPLES

A quasi-experiment was conducted in order to measure the success rate of intensive supervision participants, the program's diversionary impact, and the program's ability to ensure public safety. The experimental group consisted of all felony probationers supervised under intensive supervision from the inception of the program in December 1989, through March 1993. The average time under supervision for both groups was nearly 18 months. The comparison group consisted of a random sample of felony probationers supervised under regular probation during the same time period. Data on the population survey of IPS and the sample of regular probationers were collected from the probation department's files, and included the probationers' background characteristics, criminal history, risk assessment, and outcome status.[2] The population contained a total of 260 probationers. Of these, 166 were under intensive supervision, and 94 were supervised on regular probation.

Outcome Measures

Three measures were used to determine whether a probationer placed on IPS was classified properly. Criminal history, seriousness of offense, and risk-assessment variables were examined. Five measures were used to determine supervision outcome and were gathered at the point of program termination. Technical violations, arrests, convictions, absconder rates, and types of termination were examined. In order to develop one dependent variable, outcome was dichotomized into success or failure. Success was defined as release from supervision or still under supervision. Failure included those offenders whose probation was revoked for either a new offense, technical violation, or who absconded.

Data Analysis

The data for this study were analyzed using a number of statistical applications. Chi-square and Analysis of Variance (F test), were applied to determine whether significant differences existed between the experimental and comparison groups.[3] In addition, an attempt was made to determine the individual characteristics associated with failure. A logit analysis was performed to assist in controlling for substantive differences between the groups.

RESULTS

Background Characteristics

As shown in Table 8.1, the two groups are similar in terms of sex, race, and marital status. In both groups, approximately 85 percent are male, 97 percent are white, and 66 percent are single. However, the data indicate that there are some significant differences between the two groups. The individuals under intensive supervision were less educated than those on regular probation, and the difference is significant. This difference can be seen in Table 8.1. In addition, the two groups differ significantly in terms of employment at the time of arrest, psychiatric history, risk classification, needs classification, and presentence recommendation. The intensive supervision group was less likely to be employed at the time of arrest, more likely to have a psychiatric history, contained a higher-risk and higher-needs population than the regular probation group, and were more likely to be recommended for incarceration. The differences can be seen in Table 8.1.

Table 8.1
Background Characteristics

Variables	Intensive Probation N	%	Regular Probation N	%
Sex:				
Male	143	86	79	84
Female	23	14	15	16
Total	166	100	94	100
Race:				
Black	4	2	4	4
White	162	98	90	96
Total	166	100	94	100
Marital Status:				
Single	109	67	61	65
Married	53	33	33	35
Total	162	100	94	100
Age:				
18-21	16	10	3	3
22-28	54	33	32	24
29-35	52	32	24	26
36 & over	41	25	35	37
Total	163	100	94	100
Education:				
Less than 12	87	53	31	34
12 grade/GED	72	44	50	55
13 and up	6	4	10	11
Total	165	101	91	100
$(F = 17.7; p = .006)$	$(\bar{X} = 10.8)$		$(\bar{X} = 11.6)$	
Employed at Time of Arrest:				
Yes	81	50	67	72
No	80	50	26	28
Total	161	100	93	100
$(X^2 = 10.6; p = .001)$				

Table 8.1 *(continued)*

Variables	Intensive Probation N	%	Regular Probation N	%
Length of Residence:				
Less than 1 year	108	68	28	38
1 to 2 years	16	10	17	23
Over 2 years	35	22	29	39
Total	159	100	74	100
Psychiatric History:				
Yes	36	22	6	7
No	124	77	83	93
Total	160	99	89	100
$(X^2 = 9.0; p = .002)$				
Risk Class:				
High	66	48	8	9
Med	44	32	34	37
Low	27	20	50	54
Total	137	100	92	100
$(F = 78.2; p <.001)$	$(\bar{X} = 13.5)$		$(\bar{X} = 2.9)$	
Needs Class:				
High	46	36	10	11
Med	59	46	27	30
Low	23	18	54	59
Total	128	100	91	100
$(F = 96.9; p<.001)$	$(\bar{X} = 22.5)$		$(\bar{X} = 9.2)$	
PSI Recommendation:				
Probation	20	12	69	74
Prison	142	88	24	26
Total	162	100	93	100
$(X^2 = 96.7; p <.001)$				

N may not equal 166 and 94 due to missing data.
Percentages may not total 100% due to rounding.
Means are reported on raw scores. Date were collapsed for presentation.
Statistical tests are only reported for significant results.

Needs Assessment

The data in Table 8.2 present the results of the cross-tabulation between needs assessment and the type of supervision. As indicated above, the two groups differed significantly in terms of overall needs classification. It appears that most of the needs originate from lack of employment and lack of education. For instance, 44 percent of the intensive probation group is in need of employment assistance, compared to only 30 percent of the regular probation group. Similarly, 48 percent of the intensive group reported needing educational services, while only 29 percent of the regular cases needed the same service. Chi-square indicates that both of these findings are significant.

Table 8.2
Need Assessment Information

	Intensive Probation		Regular Probation	
Variables	N	%	N	%
Employment Services Needed:				
Yes	70	44	28	30
No	89	56	66	70
Total	159	100	94	100
$(X^2 = 4.6; p=.03)$				
Academic or Vocational Training needed:				
Yes	76	48	27	29
No	83	52	67	71
Total	159	100	94	100
$(X^2 = 8.1; p=.004)$				
Needs Assistance in Financial Management:				
Yes	34	21	21	22
No	125	79	73	78
Total	159	100	94	100
Needs Assistance in Domestic Relations:				
Yes	27	17	16	17
No	132	83	78	83
Total	159	100	94	100
Needs Assistance in Securing Suitable Living Arrangements:				
Yes	16	10	6	6
No	143	90	87	94
Total	159	100	93	100
Needs Substance Abuse Treatment:				
Yes	110	69	60	64
No	49	31	34	36
Total	159	100	94	100

N may not equal 166 and 94 due to missing data.
Percentages may not total 100% due to rounding.
Statistical tests are only reported for significant results.

Drug History

The data in Table 8.3 illustrates the differences among the two groups regarding involvement in substance abuse. Three areas resulted in significant differences. A significantly greater number of intensive probationers received prior drug treatment, were considered drug dependent, and reported being under the influence of drugs or alcohol at the time of arrest. The differences

Table 8.3
Drug History

Variables	Intensive Probation		Regular Probation	
	N	%	N	%
Drug Abuse during the Past Six Months:				
Yes	100	62	45	50
No	62	38	45	51
Total	162	100	90	100
Prior Drug Treatment:				
Yes	48	29	16	17
No	117	71	76	83
Total	165	100	92	100
$(X^2 = 3.7; p=.05)$				
Alcohol Abuse during the Past Six Months:				
Yes	100	62	45	52
No	62	38	41	48
Total	162	100	86	100
Prior Alcohol Treatment:				
Yes	53	33	23	26
No	109	67	66	74
Total	162	100	89	100
Drug Dependency:				
Yes	71	49	21	31
No	75	51	46	69
Total	146	100	67	100
$(X^2 = 20.8; p=.004)$				
Drugs/Alcohol at Time of Arrest:				
Yes	96	60	25	34
No	65	40	49	66
Total	161	100	74	100
$(X^2 = 12.5; p <.001)$				

N may not equal 166 and 94 due to missing data.
Percentages may not total 100% due to rounding.
Statistical tests are only reported for significant results.

can be seen in Table 8.3. Nearly one-half of the intensive group were drug dependent versus only 31 percent of the comparison group. Sixty-percent of the intensive cases reported having been under the influence of drugs or alcohol at the time of arrest. In comparison, only 34 percent of the regular probationers reported using drugs or alcohol at the time they were arrested.

Table 8.4
Criminal History

Variables	Intensive Probation		Regular Probation	
	N	%	N	%
Prior Felony Conviction:				
Yes	93	56	21	22
None	73	44	73	78
Total	166	100	94	100
(X^2 = 26.3; p <.001)				
Prior Felony Conviction for Violent Offense:				
Yes	20	12	9	10
No	146	88	85	90
Total	165	100	94	100
Prior Commitment in State Institution:				
Yes	72	43	9	10
No	94	57	85	90
Total	166	100	94	100
(X^2 = 30.4; p <.001)				
Prior Juvenile Record:*				
Yes	71	49	12	20
No	73	51	49	80
Total	144	100	61	100
(X^2 = 14.4; p <.001)				
Felony Level for Current Offense:**				
Felony 1	10	6	4	4
Felony 2	21	13	4	4
Felony 3	42	26	17	19
Felony 4	90	55	66	73
Total	163	100	91	100
(X^2 = 8.71; p =.03)				

N may not equal 166 and 94 due to missing data.
Percentages may not total 100% due to rounding.
   *Information pertaining to Juvenile Record was not available on 55 cases.
**A Felony 1 is the most serious and Felony 4 the least.

Criminal History

The data in Table 8.4 present the results of the cross-tabulations between criminal history and the type of supervision. The individuals under intensive supervision are clearly higher-risk than those in the regular supervision group. The intensive group were more likely to have a prior felony conviction, more likely to have a previous commitment to a state institution, had a higher percentage of individuals with a juvenile record, and were convicted of a more serious offense than the comparison sample. The differences are significant and are reported in Table 8.4.

Outcome

Four outcome measures were examined, felony arrests, felony convictions, technical violations, and current status. These data are presented in Table 8.5. The only significant finding was whether a technical violation had been filed. Thirty-nine percent of the intensive cases had an infraction that resulted in a technical violation, versus 24 percent of the regular probation sample. Other differences existed between the two groups in terms of number of felony arrests, convictions, and the current status of the offender; however, none were significant. Most probationers in both groups were classified as "successful;" however, the differences are not significant. Twenty-eight percent of the individuals under intensive supervision were revoked for committing a technical violation or a new offense, compared to 16 percent of the regular supervision group. It is difficult to determine whether the difference is due to more misconduct on the part of intensive probationers or simply the nature of the intense supervision being provided. Increased contacts and frequent random drug testing are likely to increase an intensive probationer's chances of getting caught violating the terms of probation.

Table 8.5
Current Status, Felony Arrests, and Technical Violations

| | Intensive Probation | | Regular Probation | | | |
	N	%	N	%	X^2	Sig.
Felony arrest:	13	8	4	4	.67	N.S.
Felony conviction:	12	7	4	4	.44	N.S.
Technical Violation Filed:	64	39	23	24	4.47	p=.03
Current Status of Probationer:						
Successful	113	68	75	80		
Revoked	47	28	15	16		
Other	6	4	4	6	5.02	N.S.
Total	166	101	94	100		

Table 8.6
Frequencies for Variables Predicting Program Failure

Variable	Frequency	Percent
Number of Prior Felony Convictions:		
None	138	55
1 or more	112	46
Total	250	100
Prior Juvenile Record:		
No	122	60
Yes	83	40
Total	205	100
Drug Dependency:		
No	121	57
Yes	92	43
Total	213	100
Employment Services Needed:		
No	155	61
Yes	98	39
Total	253	100
Academic Services Needed:		
No	146	60
Yes	97	40
Total	253	100
Marital Status:		
Married	85	34
Single	166	66
Total	251	100
On Drugs or Alcohol at Time of Arrest:		
No	108	48
Yes	117	52
	225	100
PSI Recommendation:		
Probation	85	35
Prison	160	65
	245	100

Mean Number of Days at Risk = 634.79
Age at Admission = 32.2
Risk Score = 9.2
Need Score = 17.2
Education Level = 11.1

N may not equal 260 due to missing data.

Section IV

CRITICAL ISSUES

And finally, whether it is electronic monitoring, boot camp, or intensive probation supervision, questions of program transferability and race will remain important concerns for everyone involved with intermediate sanctions in the 1990s. The final two chapters in this volume offer insight and direction.

With the majority of all victimizations occurring in nonmetropolitan areas, innovative intermediate sanctions designed for offenders, resources, and staff in metropolitan areas face service delivery problems in nonmetropolitan areas. The problems become more acute when small offender populations are widely distributed across large geographical areas like North Dakota and Montana. A creative solution is found in Community Corrections Boards (CCB), local volunteer groups that advise and assist government agencies with the development, implementation, and evaluation of self-supporting community corrections. The principle behind CCB and programs like it is simple; namely, the most important component of a successful community corrections program is community involvement. With that commitment in hand, rural areas can develop community volunteer programs, community service restitution programs, victim/offender mediation programs, community confinement, intensive supervision, drug offender supervision, and electronic monitoring, and adapt them to fit their unique circumstances.

And finally, when a sophisticated, longitudinal analysis, like the one that concludes this volume, demonstrates that skin color is strongly correlated with who completes residential employment-based correctional programs in relation to long-term rates of rearrest, we must wonder what it will take for residential correctional programs to reach those who need them most. Clearly, participation in residential correctional programs can have an impact on recidivism, but that impact requires successful completion. Programs everywhere must address the extent to which minorities have difficulty in successfully completing program requirements and what additional programming measures are necessary to increase the positive impact programming has on minority offenders.

9

Community Corrections
in Rural Areas:
Re-Involving the Community

Paige H. Ralph
Lake Superior State University

Richard M. Hoekstra
Division of Parole and Probation—Bismarck, ND

Timothy R. Brehm
Division of Parole and Probation—Bismarck, ND

INTRODUCTION

From 1980 to 1990, the number of inmates in state and federal institutions in the United States increased from 315,974 to 738,940. The rate of inmates per 100,000 residents also increased, from 138 to 292 (Flanagan & Maguire, 1992). Crowded prisons and limited tax dollars forced local, state, and federal governments to find and implement cost-effective and practical means of punishing criminal offenders (Maher & Dufour, 1987). Intensive supervision, house arrest, electronic monitoring, community service, and restitution have all been employed as sentencing option in a variety of states. Intensive probation supervision alone has been implemented in over 30 states (Byrne, 1986).

Many recognize the limitation of incarceration with regard to rehabilitation. Prison time removes offenders from their communities, jobs, and families and adversely affects their behavior and personality. It does not prepare them for reintegration to society. Some offenders are better served without incarceration. Community corrections programs effectively serve those offenders who do not need to be incarcerated.

RURAL VERSUS URBAN CLIENTELE

Most community corrections programs began in states with large offender populations and have come about as a response to prison overcrowding, as other chapters in this volume have shown. Most programs were located in larger urban areas in order to serve the greatest number of offenders and to take advantage of the resources available in larger urban centers. Fewer programs, however, were found in rural areas. Offenders in rural areas received probation or prison. Recently, North Dakota found a way to make a number of community corrections programs normally found in metropolitan areas available in rural areas.

North Dakota, a state with 70,665 square miles and a population of 652,695, has service delivery needs different from smaller states with denser populations. It is not uncommon for offenders to travel as many as 220 miles, round-trip, to receive the services they need or are required by the court. Required to travel over long distances makes some offenders ineligible for community-based programs. For them, the only options are probation or prison.

The North Dakota prison population is the smallest in the nation, with only 570 offenders (Flanagan & Maguire, 1992). A statistical evaluation produced by the North Dakota Division of Parole and Probation found that 14 percent of the North Dakota State Penitentiary population are violent offenders (Jenson, 1993). The remaining 86 percent could be sentenced to community corrections if programs across North Dakota were available. The rural nature of North Dakota presents a number of problems and unique opportunities for those wanting to begin community corrections programs. North Dakota's rate of probation (374 per 100,000) is the second lowest in the United States. Its rate of parole (25 per 100,000) is third lowest (Flanagan & Maguire, 1992). Probationers and parolees are dispersed throughout the state and include a significant group of Native Americans who live on reservations. Without the help of local communities, North Dakota's 35 probation and parole officers would find it impossible to provide the range of services that offenders living across the state need.

THE NORTH DAKOTA EXPERIENCE

North Dakota lagged behind most states in the development of community corrections programs. Their late arrival meant they could review what did and did not work in other states. North Dakota officials soon recognized that one of the most important components of a successful community corrections

3. Adult Parole/Probation
4. Victims Witness Assistance
5. Institutional Program
6. Human Service/Other Programs

Offender referrals to CVP are generally made by the district, county and municipal courts. The program works well with jail inmates, as well as probationers, parolees, juveniles, and potential releases. CVP existed in two cities until recently; plans for two additional programs were developed in Fiscal Year 1993.

Commuunity Service Restitution Program

The Community Service and Restitution Program (CSR) is designed to help both crime victims and offenders. Program goals include community protection, offender punishment, accountability and responsibility to victims and society. Low- to medium-risk offenders are referred to CSR by the courts to perform community service hours, to pay court costs or attorney fees, or to give restitution to crime victims. Offender noncompliance is generally handled by CSR staff who are authorized to increase an offender's community service hours or impose other conditions within limitations. Cases involving repeated noncompliance are referred back to court. CSR staff are assisted in their duties by community volunteers. Volunteers monitor offender progress in CSR programs, actively involve themselves with offenders to encourage individual, social, and vocational/educational skills and identify community placement sites. To date, volunteers in CSR have instructed youth on the proper techniques of painting, how to operate heavy machinery; transported offenders to work sites; and assisted with the supervision of offenders placed in the program.

CSR is now operating in five communities within North Dakota and more are expected to open very soon. Arguments in favor of CSR include offender service to victims or communities, a reduction in jail costs, and maintenance of employment and family support. Sixty percent of CSR clients were employed prior to sentencing and a similar percentage have at least one dependent child at home. Some offenders in CSR have obtained full-time employment at the work sites where they previously completed community service work.

Victim/Offender Mediation Program

A complimentary program of CSR across North Dakota is the Victim/Offender Mediation Program (VOMP). At present, VOMP is operating in two cities (Williston and Jamestown) in North Dakota and more programs are expected to open in 1993. North Dakota's VOMP is based on model programs operating in other cities in the United States, Canada, and Europe. Offenders and victims voluntarily agree to meet face to face. Offenders learn firsthand from the victims about the pain and damage they caused. Whether they meet once or more than once, the meeting is expected to offer the victim psychological relief. Together they agree on a plan for monetary or service restitution.

Cases are referred by the court to the community volunteer coordinator, who then prepares all the material for the mediation process and refers the case to a trained volunteer mediator. The volunteer mediator meets first with the offender, then with the victim, to explain the program. The volunteer mediator listens carefully to what their needs are and attempts to find common ground between the two. If no agreement can be reached, the case is referred back to court for disposition.

Arguments in favor of VOMP include the belief that VOMP empowers victims and gives them an opportunity to express their feelings to the offender as well as to receive answers to any lingering questions, reduces court time and expenses, fosters inclusiveness by making the victim an active participant in mediation, and gives offenders an opportunity to redress the wrong they have done and hopefully impact their future behavior.

Community Confinement and Intensive Supervision

In November 1990, the Community Confinement Program was implemented as an early release program for high-risk inmates. The program transfers prison inmates to community jails and halfway houses to serve the last 120 days of their prison sentence. The program has two goals: (1) to integrate high-risk offenders back into their communities through the use of community programs and supervision; and (2) to remove offenders from the North Dakota State Penitentiary who would be better served in community-based programming. Within months, the target population of community confinement broadened to include inmates at all risk levels, especially those sentenced to short prison terms.

The decision to release an inmate onto community confinement is made by the Warden of the North Dakota State Penitentiary with recommendations from the Penitentiary Unit Management Team and Parole Officers. Community confinement provides inmates the opportunity to find employment and build family and community ties. Supervision by a parole officer accompanies release onto community confinement. To date, no systematic evaluation of community confinement has been carried out.

In May 1991, the Intensive Supervision Program was implemented in one community to provide close supervision of high-risk offenders who would be incarcerated if not for the program. The program was introduced in a second community in April 1992. The program is available to both the North Dakota

Parole Board when it is considering parole release and the North Dakota Courts when sentencing offenders to the community.

Recommendation for intensive supervision for high-risk offenders is made by the Intensive Program Coordinator to the court or parole board. The recommendation must demonstrate that the community to which the offender is being released has resources to offer high-risk offenders. If approved by the court or parole board, the case is assigned to an ISP officer with an average caseload of 15. Technical violations for ISP cases are considered serious and may result in the offender's return or sentence to prison or extension of time under intensive supervision.

Typically, an offender on intensive supervision is required to reside at a halfway house for the first six to eight weeks. When employment and other program conditions are satisfactorily established, the offender is provided the opportunity to look for independent housing with home confinement or electronic monitoring. A minimum curfew of 10 p.m. to 6 a.m. is required of all offenders on intensive supervision. The frequency of contact with the ISP officer begins with three times per week and is reduced to once per week by the end of six months. Generally, at the end of six months on intensive supervision, offenders are transferred to regular probation caseloads.

Offender participation in intensive supervision is voluntary. During the screening phase, offenders are informed of the program's guidelines and conditions. Interestingly, shortly after intensive supervision had been in existence, some offenders felt that the program's emphasis on accountability and responsibility was not acceptable to them. They began to reject intensive supervision and serve their sentence of incarceration. However, program managers decided that once an offender knowingly and voluntarily enrolled in the program, it was not acceptable to request a sentence of incarceration.

One important learning experience of implementing intensive supervision in a rural state like North Dakota was identifying eligible cases and developing and ISP caseload. In North Dakota, it took one year to identify 15 eligible parole cases. Similarly, only one judicial district adopted intensive supervision for probationers. To counter the resistance to intensive supervision by the courts and parole board, changes are being made in the language of legislation. Currently, the program is being supported by federal grants and offender supervision fees. No systematic evaluation of intensive supervision has been carried out.

Drug Offender Caseload and On-Site Drug Testing

A federal anti-drug abuse and violent crimes grant to the North Dakota Department of Corrections and Rehabilitation provided funds to hire three probation/parole officers to work exclusively with drug offenders in the three largest communities in North Dakota. The three specialists provide high levels of supervision and surveillance to small caseloads. Simultaneously, the state also implemented on-site drug testing to screen drug offenders and provide immediate intervention. The three officers were instrumental in developing the department's policy and procedure for drug testing, detecting abuse and treatment intervention. All the department's officers statewide received training on drug testing procedures and technology to enhance their skills to manage drug offenders.

North Dakota adopted the enzyme immune assay test as a practical on-site drug test. It also preferred a lower level of drug detection to apprehend recreational use than the higher level recommended by the National Institute on Drugs of Abuse.

A significant component of the specialized drug officer's responsibilities is surveillance. The grant initially provided funding to contract with off-duty law enforcement officers to provide assistance and surveillance during evening hours. However, when the grant expired, the involvement of off-duty law enforcement officers ended. Based on the department's initial experience however, it hopes to reinvolve off-duty law enforcement officers again. No systematic evaluation of caseload specialists has been carried out.

Electronic Monitoring

Electronic monitoring program is an integral component of the Department of Corrections and Rehabilitation's intermediate conditions, community confinement, intensive supervision and drug control programs. A pilot program is underway in Devil's Lake, North Dakota. The program is based on the argument that it offers a cost-effective alternative to incarceration for state and local correctional facilities and protects the community.

Electronic monitoring will allow high-risk offenders who have demonstrated responsibility and established appropriate housing to move from a more restrictive environment such as jail or halfway house to a less restrictive home environment with an effective risk management tool. North Dakota will also pursue electronic monitoring as a sentencing option for the courts as an alternative.

The Division of Parole and Probation has selected two monitoring systems for managing felony offenders in home confinement. The first is an active monitoring system. It provides 24-hour supervision and verifies compliance with home confinement schedules through a continuous radio frequency. The second is a passive system that calls into the home and verifies an offender's presence using "an electronic handshake." Together, it is believed that these two systems will more quickly alert probation/parole officers to apparent violations in a rural state like North Dakota. Advances in the technology of electronic monitoring offer potential for statewide adoption if the pilot program is successful.

CONCLUSIONS

The commitment of the North Dakota Department of Corrections and Rehabilitation to help offenders and to try to lessen the prison population is quite unique. The department is working with a small inmate population that allows for innovative and progressive approaches to help offenders become rehabilitated.

To serve a small offender population across a very large area of land, the North Dakota Department of Corrections and Rehabilitation has involved local communities in the organization and operation of corrections programs. That approach allows for the supervision of offenders in their own communities, instead of requiring them to spend time in jail or the state penitentiary. A rural state like North Dakota has discovered that innovative correctional programs commonly found in large urban areas can be adopted to fit their needs as well. And finally, although the department has produced no systematic evaluation of the programs discussed here, expectations are high that the programs will make a difference.

10

Residential Probation Centers: The Impact of Programming and Race on Recidivism* **

Paul C. Friday
University of North Carolina—Charlotte

Robert A. Wertkin
Western Michigan University

INTRODUCTION

With prison populations at record high levels in many jurisdictions, the field of community corrections is witnessing enormous growth and development, as illustrated by the proliferation of intermediate sentences that lie on a continuum between traditional probation and imprisonment (see McCarthy, 1987; Morris & Tonry, 1990).

Residential programs or halfway houses have become integral parts of this intermediate sentencing trend. The general rationale for residential programs in community corrections is that, because of their particular risks and needs profiles, some offenders require a period of structured and supportive living if they are to function independently and successfully in the community. Program services usually center on employment and educational opportunities, substance abuse treatment, and job skill training (McCarthy & McCarthy, 1991; Smykla, 1981). Community service is frequently employed

*Revision of a paper presented at the annual meeting of the Academy of Criminal Justice Sciences, Kansas City, Missouri, March, 1993.

**The authors wish to acknowledge the cooperation and support of the Michigan Department of Corrections and express our appreciation to Bobby Brame, UNCC, who assisted with the data analysis.

as a form of societal restitution. The goal is to facilitate the integration of offenders into their local environments under the assumption that these interventions provide the requisite skills to avoid future criminality.

The program studied here, Twin Counties Probation in Three Rivers, Michigan, is a nonprofit, private organization that receives funds through the Michigan Office of Community Corrections. It is designed for male adult probationers who have been convicted of nonviolent crimes (usually felonies) and who are deemed by judges to require tighter and more structured programming than afforded by regular probation. After court screening, persons referred to the Twin Counties Community Probation Center (TCCPC) are screened for admission by the house administration.

The main emphasis of TCCPC is on the development of gainful employment and productive, responsible lifestyles by the residents. The expectation is that the residents will apply the skills they learn at the center to life outside. The program's central components include employment skills classes that are intended for individuals who are unemployed at admission and that are meant to build job-seeking and retention skills, basic life skills classes emphasizing areas like personal budgeting and preparation for and eventual obtainment of the high school equivalency diploma or GED. Other services (e.g., substance abuse counseling and vocational training) are provided for select residents through referrals to local agencies. However, the program's primary orientation is toward assisting residents in obtaining and sustaining gainful employment. All residents are required to perform a minimum of 20 hours of community service, pay court costs, and make restitution.

Client residence at TCCPC is governed by in-house and out-of-house behavior. In-house rules pertain to such things as personal hygiene and interaction with other residents. Out-of house rules govern behavior while residents are away from the facility at work, in school, or on furlough. These pertain to such things as curfews and refraining from the use of alcohol and illegal drugs. (Alcohol and drug testing are routinely conducted.) Rule compliance is monitored by staff, and attempts are made to inform the residents in advance of the potential consequences of rule violations. Violation of house rules can result in short jail terms. Following successful completion of TCCPC, which averages about five months, persons are released onto regular probation to finish the remainder of their court-imposed probation terms. This chapter investigates the question, Does participation in TCCPC impact the probability of future criminality? If so, what factors are associated with rearrest and what implications does this have for probation treatment?

METHODOLOGY

A stratified random sample of residents admitted to TCCPC from July 1, 1988 through July 1, 1991 and discharged prior to September 30, 1991 was the basis for this study. The first problem the study identified was the proportion of successful terminations. A record review showed that during the time defined for the study, there were 279 clients: 218 (78.1%) with positive releases, 55 (19.7%) with negative terminations and 6 (2.2%) listed as being terminated with "Maximum Benefit." Maximum-benefit clients were those released, prior to program completion, but who were believed to have gained as much from the program as they mentally or physically could. The sample, when statistically drawn, comprised 158 positive terminations (77.1%), 41 negative terminations (20.0%) and the six maximum-benefit clients (2.9%). The sample, therefore, is representative of the client population and was selected so as to give a sufficient "at risk" period after discharge to assess recidivism.

Data were collected from files and included basic demographic data such as age and race, legal variables such as instant offense, any jail time spent, Sentencing Guideline Score and programmatic variables such as time at Twin Counties, program participation (e.g., employment skills, substance abuse, mental health groups), and nature of discharge. Prior record information was not available with the records used for data collection.

Follow-up data were collected using the state-computerized Law Enforcement Information Network (LEIN) system in cooperation with the Michigan Department of Corrections. Since LEIN does not always provide the most comprehensive information on convictions, recidivism was defined as re-arrest. Data from the LEIN included the number and type of offense, date of offense (in terms of time "at risk" after discharge) and subsequent incarcerations. Offenders were at risk from 1 to 46 months.

Previous research has focused on factors associated with program completion (e.g., Calathes, 1991; Donnelly & Forschner, 1984; English & Mande, 1991; Moczydlowski, 1980; Moran et al., 1977; Schoen, 1972), but this research looks at these factors in relation to long-term rates of re-arrest. While studying a different population than Minor and Hartman (1992) or Hartman, Friday, and Minor (1992), it uses the same technique of long-term follow-up.

ANALYSIS

Client Characteristics

Offense. The predominant offense type was nonviolent property crimes, for which 149 (72.7 %) of the clients had been sentenced to the center. The next largest category of offense was operating a vehicle under intoxicating liquor (OUIL), for which 11 (5.4%) had been sentenced. The distribution is shown in Table 10.1.

Table 10.1
Primary Offenses

Offense	Number	Percent
Property	149	72.7
OUIL	11	5.4
Fraud/retail	10	4.9
Drugs	10	4.9
Personal	7	3.4
Probation Viol	4	2.0
Traffic	4	2.0
Weapons	3	1.5
Other	7	3.4
TOTAL	205	100.2

Jail Time. Clients at TCCPC were initially sentenced to an average of 118 days, ranging from zero to 365. On the average, they served 33 days, but the largest proportion spent no days in jail prior to entering TCCPC: 82 (40%) served no jail days; 23 (11.2%) spent one or two days in jail prior to admission in TCCPC. Three-fourths of the clients spent less than 46 jail days, but the time served ranged from 3 to 286 days. A total of 42 clients (20.5%) were given an average of 3.5 days in jail for technical violations while at TCCPC. Jail time was considered important since administrators believe that clients spending short jail terms *prior* to program participation would more likely conform to program expectations so as to avoid doing the "harder" time.

Table 10.2
Months Spent at TCCPC

Months	Number	Percent
1 month	3	1.5
2 months	21	10.2
3 months	31	15.1
4 months	46	22.4
5 months	60	29.3
6 months	23	11.2
7 months	7	3.4
8 months	7	3.4
9 months	2	1.0
10 months	4	2.0
11 months	1	0.5
TOTAL	205	100.0

Months at TCCPC. For programming to have an impact, it was assumed to require adjustment time. The average length of stay at Twin Counties was 5 months, suggesting that administrators felt they had provided their services by this time. The range was from 1 to 11 months with the largest proportion (29.3%) staying five months. Cumulatively, 78.5 percent stayed five months or less (see Table 10.2). Twenty-one clients (10.2%) went AWOL from the program and were considered as having had negative terminations.

Age. The average age of the client population at Twin Counties was 21.2 years. The range was from 17 (11.2%) to 44 (0.5%) with the largest proportion being 18 years old (28.33%). Slightly over one-half of the population (54.1%) was 17 to 19 at the time of commitment to Twin Counties. This residential program is, therefore, designed to be a critical early intervention in a potential criminal career.

Race. TCCPC serves, primarily, a white clientele. By race, 180 (87.8%) were white while 18 (8.8%) were African-American; other races constituted 3.4 percent (N=7).

Education. Information on the number of years of school completed was not available on all clients. But for those for whom it was known, about two-thirds (69.6%) had not completed high school. Of these, 10.6 percent had completed school only through eighth grade. Those completing high school (or indicated possession of a GED) numbered 46 (28.6%). Only three clients had post high school education.

Alcohol/Drugs. Alcohol and drug abuse problems were identified as part of the presentence process and notations were made on the files. In 40.5 percent (N=83) of the cases, there was notation of an alcohol abuse problem; in 27.8 percent (N=57) a drug problem was noted.

Table 10.3
TCCPC Programming Summary

	Numbers/Percent of Sample	
Employment Training Services	184	(89.8)
Substance Abuse Services	155	(75.6)
Training/Educ. Placement Serv.	92	(44.9)
Housing Services	15	(7.3)
Community Service	200	(97.6)
Job Seeking Skills	95	(46.3)
Work Release	11	(5.4)
Employment Search	146	(71.2)

TCCPC Program Participation. The following is an indication of the number of clients recorded as having participated in the range of TCCPC programming. It was of interest to this study which program components would be related to either program success or related to recidivism. Clients could be in more than one program.

While the mandatory number of community service hours is 20, the average number of hours of community service was 37.8, with the most frequent number being 20. The range was from zero hours (N=7) to 205 hours (N=1).

TCCPC Program Termination. The sample was specifically stratified to represent the known population distribution: 158 (77.1%) were classified as having been positively terminated; 41 (20.0%) were listed as negative terminations while six clients were designated as having received "Maximum Benefit" from the program, meaning that staff considered the client incapable of gaining anything more from further participation in the program.

FINDINGS

Re-Arrest Prevalence

Re-Arrest Record. Using the Michigan State LEIN system, a total of 84 TCCPC clients (41.0%) were arrested after release from the program. Sixty-two (73.8%) were arrested for new felonies; 12 (14.3%) for only misdemeanor charges, 3 (3.6%) with traffic offenses, and the remaining 7 (8.3%) had a combination of charges.

Six clients (7.1%) were rearrested within the first year of discharge from TCCPC; all of these arrests occurred within the first six months of release. Within two years after discharge, an additional 24 (28.6%) of those who were eventually re-arrested, were charged. During the third year after discharge, another 32 (38%) were rearrested and the remainder (22) were rearrested within the study's 46-month framework.

Type of Offense. Nearly one-half (47.6%) of the reoffending population was charged with property crimes. The second largest category was drugs (14.6%)—proportionately higher than the five percent initially charged with drug offenses. The distribution is as shown in Table 10.4.

Table 10.4
First Rearrest Charges

Property	40	47.6%
Drugs	12	14.3%
Personal	8	9.5%
Traffic	7	8.3%
Fraud/Retail	6	7.1%
OUIL	5	6.0%
Other	6	7.1%
TOTAL	84	99.9%

FACTORS ASSOCIATED WITH THE
PREVALENCE OF RE-ARREST

Of the offenders studied, 41 percent were rearrested. The following variables were associated with re-arrest:

1. The most significant factor associated with re-arrest was months in the program. The longer the stay, the greater the likelihood of successful completion of the program and the less the likelihood of re-arrest. Clients spending more than three months in the program were significantly less likely to be re-arrested ($X^2 = 37.45$, df=1, p < .001).

2. Offenders with a positive termination from the program were significantly less likely to fail than offenders with a negative termination status ($X^2 = 25.42$, df=1, p < .001).

3. Whites were less likely to be re-arrested than nonwhites ($X^2 = 11.33$, df=1, p < .002). But when program termination status (positive or negative) is controlled, the race/re-arrest relationship is not significant although the direction is worth noting. For those positively terminated, 50 percent of the nonwhites are re-arrested compared with 29.4 percent of the whites. For those negatively terminated, 70 percent of the whites were re-arrested and 91 percent of the nonwhites. This may be a function of a small sample.

4. Serving jail time (for a technical violation while in the program) was positively related to re-arrest ($X^2 = 5.71$, df=1, p < .02).

5. Alcohol use was positively associated with failure but only in the presence of certain control variables. By itself, the relationship between alcohol abuse and re-arrest was insignificant ($X^2 = 1.33$, df=1, p < .25). But, known alcohol abusers were twice as likely to be rearrested than non-abusers in one special group: those who had been at risk the 14 to 33 months and who had also received a positive or maximum benefit termination (N=95).

6. Time at risk was positively related to re-arrest. The analysis identified three cohesive groups: 1 to 14 months, 15 to 33 months, and 34+ months. The longer the elapsed time from release, the greater the probability of re-arrest. ($X^2 = 22.35$, df=2, p < .003).

A multiple logistic regression model was estimated with re-arrest as the criterion. Time at risk, termination status, alcohol use, jail time, and race were forced in the model.

The logistic regression results (Maximum Likelihood Analysis) are shown in Table 10.5. Figure 10.1, using a chi-square based automatic interaction detection procedure, CHAID, (Kass, 1980) illustrates the interaction effect determined from the regression analysis. The results suggest that time at risk is critical in re-arrest with the cut-off period being 14 months. Of those who were within one year of release, and likely to be on continued probation, only 3.7 were rearrested. But of those 14 through 33 months, 41 percent were rearrested and 57 percent of those who had been out of the program more than three years were rearrested.

Table 10.5
Model Summary: Maximum Likelihood Analysis

Variable	Parameter Estimate	Standard Error	Chi-Square	p
Intercept	−5.0866	0.8934	32.4150	< .001
RISKTIME	0.7136	0.2597	7.5523	< .006
TERMSTAT	1.3730	0.4291	10.2379	< .002
ALCOHOL	0.4359	0.3304	1.7414	< .187
JAIL	0.4950	0.3994	1.5362	< .215
RACE	1.1109	0.5146	4.6600	< .031
−2 Log Likelihood X^2 = 42.41, df = 5, p < .001				

The difference in rates of re-arrest are shown in Figure 10.1 to be influenced by program termination type. Of those negatively terminated within the long-term release group 83 percent were re-arrested while approximately one-third of those positively released from the program for over 14 months were rearrested. It is for this group that known alcohol abuse was a factor.

Race did not enter into the equation when time at risk and type of program termination were controlled, but it was found to be a factor in whether one successfully completed the program.

Variables Associated with Program Termination Status

Since program termination status is an important factor in future arrests, the variables associated with successful program completion must be analyzed. Cross tabulations revealed three variables to be significantly related to positive termination from TCCPC: number of months in the program, race, and successful employment search.

1. As months in the program increased, the greater the likelihood of a positive termination. Table 10.6 shows the strongest differences in months were detected when they were collapsed to 1 to

    2 months, 3 to 4 months, and 5 to 11 months ($X^2 = 80.33$, df = 4, p < .001).

2. Whites were more likely to have positive terminations than non-whites as seen in Table 10.7. (p < .002).

3. As seen in Table 10.8, evidence of a successful employment search was significantly associated with a higher prevalence of positive terminations and lower prevalence of maximum benefit and negative terminations ($X^2 = 24.35$ df = 2, p. < .0001).

Months in TCCPC. Those who spent 1 to 2 months in the program, 66.7 percent were terminated as negative. Of those in the program 4 to 5 months, 31.7 percent were terminated as negative. And only 9.8 percent of those spending six months or more in the program were terminated as negative.

Table 10.6
Months in TCCPC and Termination

	1-2 months		3-4 months		5-11 months	
Positive	3	(12.5%)	59	(76.6%)	96	(92.3%)
Max/Ben	5	(20.8%)	1	(1.3%)		
Negative	16	(66.6%)	17	(22.1%)	8	(7.7%)
	24		77		104	

$X^2 = 80.33$, df = 4, p <.001

Table 10.7
Race and TCCPC Termination

	White		Nonwhite	
Positive	146	(81.1%)	12	(48.0%)
Max/Ben	4	(2.2%)	2	(8.0%)
Negative	30	(16.7%)	13	(44.0%)
	180		25	

$X^2 = 13.83$, df = 2, p < .002

Table 10.8
Successful Employment Search

	Yes		No	
Positive	150	(82.6%)	8	(36.4%)
Max/Ben	5	(2.7%)	1	(4.5%)
Negative	28	(15.3%)	13	(59.1%)
	183		22	

$X^2 = 24.35$, df = 2, p < .0001

Successful employment search, however, is not statistically related to race. The chi-square distribution is shown in Table 10.9. While 22 percent of non-whites were not successful in their searches and 9 percent of whites were unsuccessful, chi-square significance is only .09 and Fisher's Exact Test is .10. The small N for nonwhites may be a factor here.

Table 10.9
Employment Search and Race

	White		Nonwhite	
Not Successful	17	(9.4%)	4	(22.2%)
Successful	163	(90.6%)	14	(77.8%)

$X^2 = 2.817$, df=1, p< .09

Using CHAID (Kass, 1980), which uses a built-in significance test and identifies the most significant predictor, Figure 10.2 shows race to be the strongest factor in termination success. For nonwhites, none of the other factors, including employment search, seem to play a role. For whites, time in the program is important. If in the program one or two months, 62.5 percent are terminated negatively while only 7.1 percent receive negative terminations if they remain in the program five or more months.

Successful employment search plays a role for those in the program three or four months. For those who find jobs, 86 percent are released with a positive termination while two-thirds of those who do not find jobs are released negatively.

One variable entered the picture as being related to the termination status of the 98 clients who were in the program five or more months. Clients who were sent to jail during their stay (usually for a short-term and for a technical probation violation) were more likely to be negatively terminated after five months than those who did not go to jail. However, this variable is important only for this subset of white clients.

SUMMARY AND DISCUSSION

This analysis suggests that a few factors weigh heavily on the future recidivism of offenders sentenced to residential probation. While generally young, residential probation clients are not usually first offenders and have generally spent some time in jail. Residential probation is viewed as a last, stopgap measure in reducing the chances for a long-term criminal career. These data show that failure to successfully complete the program is statistically related to future re-arrest.

Time at risk to recidivate and program termination type were the strongest factors related to recidivism while race, time in the program and successful employment search were, in turn, related to successful termination. While two-way cross tabulations would suggest that nonwhite clients, all else being equal, were almost twice as likely to be re-arrested as whites, the impact of race is mitigated by program completion. Similarly, those receiving a negative termination are more than twice as likely to be re-arrested than those terminating positively.

The importance of these findings is that participation in residential probation programs can have an impact on recidivism, but that impact requires successful completion. However, there is some indication that nonwhites are less likely to successfully complete the program.

These data are consistent with Moczydlowski's (1980) claim that variables which are predictive of in-program performance are not necessarily predictive of post-program performance. The data are also consistent with Donnelly and Forschner's (1984) contention that in-program success should be associated with lower rates of post-program recidivism.

Program completion, itself, is more important than completion of any of the individual program components, with the possible exception of successful employment searches, for future arrest rates. Program termination status, then, should be seen as having a summary or cumulative effect and incorporating variables not measured by assessment of individual program components such as community service, drug treatment, or education/training. Programming must be seen as a package, the successful completion of which may be influenced by such unmeasured variables as program usefulness in meeting the needs of the offender, client motivation for change, and the amenability of clients to respond to program expectations. The dynamics associated with successful termination are greater than the specific program components.

CONCLUSION

Residential probation can impact future criminal behavior, but one must successfully complete the program. However, apparent positive effects of successful completion must be tempered by the fact that there is a differential rate of successful completion by nonwhites and that the value of successful completion is less as the period of time from program termination increases. Five points stand out in this analysis:

1. There is a racial difference in the rate of successful program termination and that failure to successfully complete the program increases the rate of re-arrest.

Interpretation of the race effect is difficult. One cannot say why the racial effect is so strong relative to successful termination. It may be a function of the small sample size. But similar research (Minor & Hartman, 1992; Hartmann, Friday & Minor, 1992) showed the racial factor to remain significant, independent of termination status, for re-arrest after a seven-year follow-up. The racial differences need to be more systematically addressed. Some may interpret such findings as being related to systematic discrimination or to the criminogenic influences of a ghetto environment. These data cannot reveal the underlying reasons. However, successful program completion is critical; future research should be directed, therefore, toward determining if residential programs are meeting the needs of all clients, especially nonwhite clients. A related question is whether nonwhite clients are amenable to the programs being offered by residential probation centers. Successful program completion, like completion of higher education, may not have the same value within the minority peer subculture as it would appear to have for those who developed the program (See *Charlotte Observer* (NC), 1993).

On the basis of the data analysis one can say, however, that statistical control for age, education, employment, juvenile and adult record, history of drug or alcohol abuse, and a variety of other factors, does not explain the differential success of nonwhite and white subjects. However, the strong relationship between successful employment search and positive program termination may make it more difficult for nonwhites since the job opportunities in an economically depressed state such as Michigan may not be available. The racial factor may be, quite simply, an economic market factor.

2.   The effect of probation programming, especially employment training/search, wanes after the clients have been away from the program or go off nonresidential probation that might monitor the employment.

Correctional programs can be expected to be influential for a limited amount of time and if there is no social or family support structure to reinforce the precepts of the programming, it becomes a matter of time before the conditions that may have influenced the initial involvement in crime are once again strong and influential. The 14-month time period before major failures occur suggests that clients may, in fact, be attempting to remain free of crime involvement; what makes this a crucial time frame needs to be investigated since it is not clear if re-arrest coincides with the termination of probation supervision.

3.   Alcohol abuse, if not successfully addressed, continues to play a role in future re-arrests even for those who successfully complete the program.

Involvement in alcohol treatment programs never statistically surfaced as important in either program completion or re-arrest, but having entered the program with an alcohol (but not drug) abuse problem had lingering effects, especially as the risk period increased. This indirectly supports the need to address the long-term support structure of clients.

4. Given the impact of time, intervening factors such as interpersonal and/or economic changes may be impacting the motivation or opportunity to maintain a lifestyle that is crime preventive.

This point is only speculative and clearly goes beyond the scope of the data. But the implication is clear. Correctional programming, even for those who successfully complete it, has its limits and policymakers may need to think of longer-term support structures.

5. The rate of successful termination should be addressed. Since successful termination was associated with a reduced probability of recidivism during the follow-up period, it would seem desirable to minimize the number of unsuccessfully terminated persons while maximizing the number of successful terminations.

An 80 percent rate of successful termination is high. Perhaps too high and a reflection of some form of net widening. This is not an issue addressed in this study, but the nature of the client population should be of major concern. While increasing the rate of successful completions is important, net widening needs to be avoided and the admission criteria used by the courts and house administration to determine which probationers were likely to benefit from and succeed in residential probation need to be considered vis-à-vis program structure and substance. The prospects of maximizing the rate of successful terminations must be done by looking at client needs, especially minority needs, and finding ways to impact the amenability of clients to programming. Further research is important to determine which offenders are and are not likely to benefit from specific correctional programs (see Bonta & Motiuk, 1985; Orsagh & Marsden, 1985).

Successful completion of the Twin Counties Community Probation Center program appears to be significantly related to clients not becoming reinvolved in crime. Successful or positive termination from the program appears to be a factor when all other variables are considered. So while the rate of rearrest for program participants as a whole is around 40 percent, the rate for those positively terminated is significantly better than for those negatively terminated. Since none of the specific program components differentiated between later criminality and noncriminality, program participation and program completion in and of itself may offer clients the needed element of success for future crime-free behavior but may not significantly change the proclivities of serious offenders.

Termination success is related to race and time in the program, but termination type is more significant than race in later involvement in crime. This suggests that future crime can be impacted by increasing the number of minority clients successfully completing the program. Since race is significantly related to positive program completion and is related to re-arrest only if minority clients are negatively terminated, the program should address the extent to which minorities have difficulty in successfully completing the program requirements and whether additional programming measures may be necessary to increase the positive impact programming has on minority offenders.

Positive completion of the program appears to have relatively long-term impact. The low rate of recidivism within the first year is remarkable. Later recidivist activity may be due to a host of other social, economic, or demographic factors unrelated to program participation. Looking at both the minority issue and the reinvolvement in crime after considerable time lapse suggests that factors outside of the program's control are operative. Overall, the program can be seen to have a very positive impact on those clients who successfully complete it, and this impact is long-term.

Figure 10.1
Inter-Relationship of Variables Related to Recidivism Record

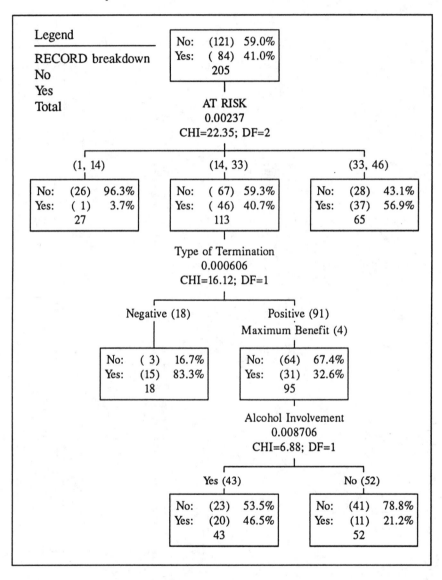

Figure 10.2
Inter-Relationship of Variables Related to Recidivism Record

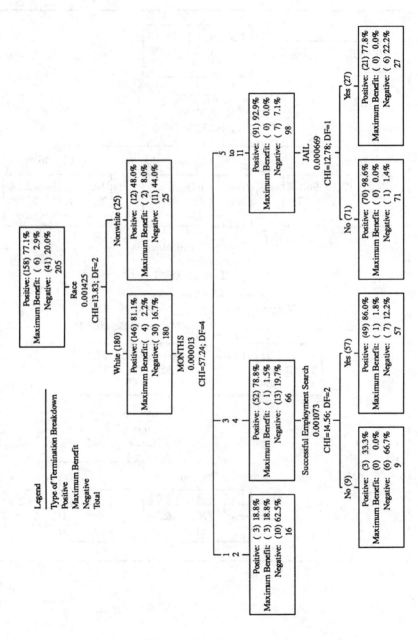

Bibliography

Abt Associates (1991, April). "Georgia Boot Camp Sidebar."

Ahlbrandt, R.S. & J.V. Cunningham (1979). *A New Public Policy for Neighborhood Preservation.* New York, NY: Praeger.

Aldrich, J. & F. Nelson (1984). *Linear Probability, Logit, and Probit Models.* Beverly Hills, CA: Sage.

American Correctional Association (1990). *Intermediate Punishment: Community-Based Sanctions.* Baltimore, MD: United Book Press.

Andrews, D.A., J. Bonta & R.D. Hoge (1990). "Classification for Effective Rehabilitation: Rediscovering Psychology." *Criminal Justice and Behavior,* 17 (1):19-52.

Andrews, D.A., I. Zinger, R.D. Hoge, J. Bonta, P. Gendreau & F.T. Cullen (1990). "Does Correctional Treatment Work? A Clinically Relevant and Psychologically Informed Meta-Analysis." *Criminology,* 28(3):369-404.

Anglin, M.D. & Y. Hser (1990). "Treatment of Drug Abuse." In M. Tonry & J.Q. Wilson (eds.), *Crime and Justice: Drugs and Crime,* pp. 355-375. Chicago, IL: University of Chicago.

"APPA Issues Committee Report" (1991). *Perspectives,* 15:34-36.

Austin, J. & B. Krisberg (1982). "The Unmet Promise of Alternatives to Incarceration." *Crime and Delinquency,* 28:374-409.

Baird, S.C. & D. Wagner (1990). "Measuring Diversion: The Florida Community Control Program." *Crime and Delinquency,* 36:112-125.

Ball, R., C. Huff & J. Lilly (1988). *House Arrest and Correctional Policy: Doing Time at Home.* Newbury Park, CA: Sage.

Banks, J., A.L. Porter, R.L. Rardin, R.R. Sider & V.E. Unger (1976). *Evaluation of Intensive Special Probation Projects: Phase I Report* (Grant No. 76 NI-99-0045). Washington, DC: U.S. Department of Justice.

Bartollas, C. (1985). *Correctional Treatment: Theory and Practice*. Englewood Cliffs, NJ: Prentice-Hall.

Baumer, T., R. Mendelsohn & C. Rhine (1990). *Final Report: The Electronic Monitoring of Nonviolent Convicted Felons: An Experiment in Home Detention*. Washington, DC: U.S. Department of Justice, National Institute of Justice.

Bazemore, G. (1992). "On Mission Statements and Reform in Juvenile Justice: The Case of the 'Balanced Approach.'" *Federal Probation*, LVI(3):64-70.

Benekos, P.J. (1990). "Beyond Reintegration: Community Corrections in a Retributive Era." *Federal Probation*, LIV(1):52-56.

Blomberg, T., G. Waldo & L. Burcroff (1987). "Home Confinement and Electronic Surveillance." In B.R. McCarthy (ed.) *Intermediate Punishments: Intensive Supervision, Home Confinement and Electronic Surveillance*. New York, NY: Willow Tree Press, Inc.

Blumstein, A. (1982). "On the Racial Disproportionality of United States Prison Populations." *Journal of Criminal Law and Criminology*, 73(3):1260-1281.

Bonta, J. & L.L. Motiuk (1985). "Utilization of an Interview-Based Classification Instrument: A Study of Correctional Halfway Houses." *Criminal Justice and Behavior*, 12:333-352.

Braswell, M.C. (1989). "Correctional Treatment and the Human Spirit: A Focus on Relationship." *Federal Probation*, LIII(2):49-60.

Bureau of Census (1990). Publication of U.S. Dept. of Commerce, Census of Population and Housing, Summary of Social, Economic and Housing Characteristics. Washington, DC: U.S. Government Printing Office.

_____ (July, 1992). *National Update*. Washington, DC: U.S. Government Printing Office.

_____ (1992). *National Update* (NCJ-133097). Washington, DC: U.S. Department of Justice.

Burke, P.B. (1990). "Classification and Case Management for Probation and Parole: Don't Shoot the Messenger." *Perspectives*, 14(3):37-42.

Burkhart, W.R. (1986). "Intensive Probation Supervision: An Agenda for Research and Evaluation." *Federal Probation*, 50(2):75-77.

Byrne, J.M. (1986). "The Control Controversy: A Preliminary Examination of Intensive Probation Supervision in the United States." *Federal Probation*, 50(2):4-16.

_____ (1989). "Reintegrating the Concept of Community into Community-Based Corrections," *Crime and Delinquency*, 35:471-497.

_____ (1990). "The Future of Intensive Probation Supervision and the New Intermediate Sanctions." *Crime and Delinquency*, 36 (January):6-41.

Byrne, J.M. & L. Kelly (1989). *Restructuring Probation as an Intermediate Sanction: An Evaluation of the Massachusetts Intensive Probation Supervision Program. Final Report to the National Institute of Justice, Research Program on the Punishment and Control of Offenders*. Washington, DC: U.S. Department of Justice.

Byrne, J.M, A.J. Lurigio & S.C. Baird (1989). "The Effectiveness of the New Intensive Supervision Programs." *Research in Corrections*, 2(2):1-48.

_____ (1989). "The Effectiveness of the New Intensive Supervision Programs." *Research in Corrections*, 5:1-70.

Calathes, W. (1991). "Project Green Hope, a Halfway House for Women Offenders." *Journal of Contemporary Criminal Justice*, 7:136-145.

Carter, R.M. (1967). "The Presentence Report and the Decision-Making Process." *Journal of Research in Crime and Delinquency*, 4:203-211.

Carter, R. & L.T. Wilkins (1976). "Caseloads: Some Conceptual Models." In R. Carter & L.T. Wilkins (eds.) *Probation, Parole and Community Corrections*, pp. 391-401. New York, NY: Wiley & Sons, Inc.

Champion, D.J. (1988). *Felony Probation: Problems and Prospects*. New York, NY: Praeger.

Charles, M.T. (1989). "Electronic Monitoring for Juveniles." *Journal of Crime and Justice*, 12(2):147-169.

Charlotte Observer (1993). February 27, p. E1.

Clarkson, J.S. & J.J. Weakland (1991). "A Transitional Aftercare Model for Juveniles: Adapting Electronic Monitoring and Home Confinement." *Journal of Offender Monitoring*, 4(2):2-15.

Clear, T.R. (1986). *JIPS: Theory and Rationale*. Paper presented at JIPS Symposium co-sponsored by Hennepin County Juvenile Court and National Council of Juvenile and Family Court Judges.

_____ (1988). "Statistical Prediction in Corrections." *Research in Corrections*, 1:1-40.

_____ (1988). *Research in Corrections*. Washington, DC: U.S. Department of Justice, National Institute of Corrections.

Clear, T.R., V.B. Clear & W.D. Burrell (1989). *Offender Assessment and Evaluation: The Presentence Investigation Report*. Cincinnati, OH: Anderson Publishing Co.

Clear, T.R., S. Flynn, C. Shapiro & E. Latessa. "Intensive Supervision in Probation: A Comparison of Three Projects." In B. McCarthy (ed.) *Intermediate Punishments: Intensive Supervision, Home Confinement and Electronic Surveillance*, pp. 31-50. Monsey, NY: Willow Tree Press.

Clear, T.R. & P.L. Hardyman (1990). "The New Intensive Supervision Movement." *Crime and Delinquency*, 36:42-60.

Clear, T.R. & E.J. Latessa (1993). "Probation Officer Roles in Intensive Supervision: Surveillance versus Treatment." *Justice Quarterly*, 10:(3).

Clear, T.R. & V. O'Leary (1983). *Controlling the Offender in the Community*. Lexington, MA: Lexington Books.

Clements, C.B. (1986). *Offender Needs Assessment*. College Park, MD: American Correctional Association.

Cochran, D. (1989). "A Practitioner's Perspective." *Research in Corrections*, 2:57-63.

Cochran, D., R.P. Corbett & J.M. Byrne (1986). "Intensive Probation Supervision in Massachusetts: A Case Study in Change." *Federal Probation*, L(2):32-41.

Colson, C. & D.W. Van Ness (1989). "Alternatives to Incarceration." *The Journal of State Government*, 62(2):59-64.

Coyle, E.J. (1990). *Boot Camp Prisons*. Newark, NJ: Criminal Disposition Commission.

Cullen, F. & P. Gendreau (1988). "The Effectiveness of Correctional Rehabilitation." In L. Goodstein & D.L. MacKenzie (eds.) *The American Prison: Issues in Research Policy*, pp. 23-43. New York, NY: Plenum.

De Luca, H.R., T.J. Miller & C.F. Wiedemann (1991). "Punishment vs. Rehabilitation: A Proposal for Revising Sentencing Practices." *Federal Probation*, LV(3):37-45.

Dillon, W.R. & M. Goldstein (1984). *Multivariate Analysis: Methods and Applications*. New York, NY: John Wiley & Sons.

Donnelly, P.G. & B. Forschner (1984). "Client Success or Failure in a Halfway House." *Federal Probation*, 48:38-44.

Editor, *Journal of Offender Monitoring* (1990). "Monitoring Juvenile Offenders: The Kenosha County Wisconsin Experience." *Journal of Offender Monitoring*, 3(3):2-7.

Eisenberg, M. & G. Markley (1987). "Something Works in Community Supervision." *Federal Probation*, LI(4):28-32.

Elis, L.A., D.L. MacKenzie & C.C. Souryal (1992). "Boot Camp Prisons: A Growing Trend in Corrections." Unpublished paper.

English, K.K. & M.J. Mande (1991). "Empirical Support for Intervention Strategies in Community Corrections." *Journal of Contemporary Criminal Justice*, 7:95-106.

Erwin, B.S. (1987). *Final Report: Evaluation of Intensive Probation Supervision in Georgia*. Atlanta, GA: Georgia Department of Corrections.

———— (1990). "Old and New Tools for the Modern Probation Officer." *Crime and Delinquency*, 36:61-74.

Farrell, M.J. (1988). "The Development of the Community Patrol Officer Program: Community Oriented Policing in the New York City Police Department." In J.R. Greene & S.D Mastrofski (eds.) *Community Policing: Rhetoric or Reality*, pp. 73-88. New York, NY: Praeger.

Flanagan, T. & K. Maguire (eds.) (1992). *Sourcebook of Criminal Justice Statistics, 1991*. Washington, DC: U.S. Department of Justice, Bureau of Justice Statistics.

Florida Department of Corrections, Bureau of Planning, Research, and Statistics (1989). *Research Report: Boot Camp Evaluation*. Tallahassee, FL.

———— (1990). *Florida Executive Summary: Boot Camp: A 25-Month Review*. Tallahassee, FL: Author.

Florida Department of Corrections (1990). "Boot Camp: A Twenty-Five Month Review." Tallahassee, FL: Unpublished report.

Flowers, G.T., T.S. Carr & R.B. Ruback (1991). *Special Alternative Incarceration Evaluation*. Atlanta, GA: Georgia Department of Corrections.

Fogg, V. (1992). "Implementation of a Cognitive Skills Development Program." *Perspectives*, 16(1):24-26.

Fried, M. (1984). "The Structure and Significance of Community Satisfaction." *Population and Environment*, 7:61-86.

Friel, C. & J. Vaughn (1986). "A Consumers Guide to the Electronic Surveillance of Probationers." *Federal Probation Quarterly*, L(3):3-14.

Friel, C.M., J.B. Vaughn & R. del Carmen (1987). *Electronic Monitoring and Correctional Policy: The Technology and Its Application*. Washington, DC: National Institute of Justice.

Fyfe, J.J. (1991). "Some Hard Facts About Our Wars on Crime." *Washington Post National Weekly*, 24(April):8-14.

Gendreau, P. (1993). "Principles of Effective Intervention." In *A New Direction for Intensive Supervision*. Lexington, KY: American Probation and Parole Association.

Gendreau, P. & D.A. Andrews (1990). "Tertiary Prevention: What the Meta-Analyses of the Offender Treatment Literature Tell Us About 'What Works.'" *Canadian Journal of Criminology*, 32:173-184.

Gendreau, P., D.A. Andrews, C. Goggin & F. Chanteloupe (1992). *The Development of Clinical and Policy Guidelines for the Prediction of Criminal Behavior in Criminal Justice Settings* (Contract No. 1514-UNO-4200). Report to the Corrections Branch, Ministry Secretariat, Solicitor General of Canada.

Gendreau, P. & R.R. Ross (1987). "Revivification of Rehabilitation: Evidence from the 1980s." *Justice Quarterly*, 4:349-407.

Georgia Department of Corrections (1991). "Special Alternative Incarceration: Evaluation." Atlanta, GA: Unpublished report.

Gettinger, S. (1984). "Assessing Criminal Justice Needs." *National Institute of Justice Research in Brief*. Rockville, MD: National Criminal Justice Reference Service.

Gibbons, D.C. (1988). *The Limits of Punishment as Social Policy*. San Francisco, CA: National Council on Crime and Delinquency.

Glaser, D. & M. Gordon (1990). "Profitable Penalties for Lower Level Courts," *Judicature*, 73:248-252.

Glaser, D. & R. Watts (1992a). *An Experiment in House Arrest With Electronic Monitoring for Drug Criminals on Probation*. A reported submitted to the National Institute of Justice, U.S. Department of Justice, Grant No. 90-IJ-CX-0005.

_____ (1992b). "Electronic Monitoring of Drug Offenders on Probation" *Judicature*, 76(October-November):112-117.

Goss, M. (1989). "Electronic Monitoring: The Missing Link for Successful House Arrest." *Corrections Today*, 53(July):106,108.

Greenberg, S.W. & W.M. Rohe (1986). "Informal Social Control and Crime Prevention in Modern Urban Neighborhoods." In R.B. Taylor (ed.) *Urban Neighborhoods: Research and Policy*, pp. 79-118. New York, NY: Praeger.

Greenfeld, L.A. (1990). *Prisoners in 1989*. Washington, DC: U.S. Department of Justice.

Greenwod, P.W. (1984). "Selective Incapacitation: A Method of Using Our Prisons More Effectively." *National Institute of Justice Reports*, (January):4-7.

Hahn, P. (n.d.). "Are Boot Camps Really the Answer?" Unpublished manuscript, Xavier University, Department of Criminal Justice, Cincinnati, Ohio.

Harland, A.T. & C.J. Rosen (1987). "Sentencing Theory and Intensive Supervision Probation." *Federal Probation*, LI(4):33-42.

Hartmann, D., P.C. Friday & K.I. Minor (1992). "Residential Probation: A Seven Year Follow-up Study of Halfway House Discharges." Paper presented at the meeting of the Southern Criminal Justice Association, Gatlinburg, Tennessee.

Hirschi, T. (1969). *Causes of Delinquency.* Berkeley, CA: University of California Press.

Hudson, J. & B. Galaway (1990). "Community Service: Toward Program Definition." *Federal Probation,* LIV(2):3-9.

Hylton, J.H. (1982). "Rhetoric and Reality: A Critical Appraisal of Community Correctional Programs." *Crime and Delinquency* 28:341-373.

Illinois Department of Corrections, Planning and Research (1992). *Impact Incarceration Program: 1992 Annual Report to the Governor and the General Assembly.* Springfield, IL.

Irwin, J. & J. Austin (1987). *It's About Time: Solving America's Prison Crowding Problem.* San Francisco, CA: National Council on Crime and Delinquency.

Jenson, C. (1993). *Inmate Records Summary Report.* Bismarck, ND: North Dakota State Penitentiary.

Jolin, A. & B. Stipak (1992). "Drug Treatment and Electronically Monitored Home Confinement: An Evaluation of a Community-Based Sentencing Option." *Crime and Delinquency,* 38(April):158-170.

Johnson, R. (1987). *Hard Time: Understanding and Reforming the Prison.* Monterey, CA: Brooks/Cole.

Johnson, G. & R.M. Hunter (1992). "Evaluation of the Specialized Drug Offender Program for the Colorado Judicial Department." Unpublished manuscript, Center for Action Research University of Colorado at Boulder.

Jones, M. (1991). "Intensive Probation Supervision in Georgia, Massachusetts, and New Jersey." *Criminal Justice Research Bulletin.* Sam Houston State University, Huntsville, TX: 6(1):1-9.

Jones, P.R. (1990). "Community Corrections in Kansas: Extending Community-Based Corrections or Widening the Net?" *Journal of Research in Crime and Delinquency,* 27:79-101.

Juvenile Center (1991). *Superior Court of Lake County Juvenile Division Annual Report.* Gary, IN: Juvenile Court Probation Department.

Kass, G.V. (1980). "An Exploratory Technique for Investigating Large Quantities of Categorical Data." *Applied Statistics,* 29:119-127.

Kelsey, R. (1991). *Bucks County Adult Probation Department Intensive Supervision Program: Four-Year Report.* Bucks County, PA.

Kramer, J.H. & R.L. Lubitz (1985). "Pennsylvania's Sentencing Reform: The Impact of Commission-Established Guidelines." *Crime and Delinquency,* 31:481-500.

Kuplinski, J. (1990). *Electronic Offender Monitoring in Virginia: Evaluation Report.* Richmond, VA: Department of Criminal Justice Services, Division of State and Local Services, Correctional Services Section.

Latessa, E. (1986). "Cost Effectiveness of Intensive Supervision." *Federal Probation,* 50(2):70-74.

Lawrence, R. (1991). "Reexamining Community Corrections Models." *Crime and Delinquency,* 37:449-464.

Lewis, D.A. & G. Salem (1981). "Community Crime Prevention: An Analysis of a Developing Perspective." *Crime and Delinquency,* 27:405-421.

Lilly, J., B. Ball & J. Wright (1987). "Home Incarceration with Electronic Monitoring in Kenton County, Kentucky: An Evaluation." In B.R. McCarthy (ed.) *Intermediate Punishments: Intensive Supervision, Home Confinement and Electronic Surveillance,* pp. 189-203, Monsey, NY: Willow Tree Press, Inc.

Lipchitz, J.W. (1986). "Back to the Future: An Historical View of Intensive Probation Supervision." *Federal Probation,* L(2):78-81.

Louisiana Department of Public Safety and Corrections (1992). IMPACT: A Program of the Louisiana Department of Public Safety and Corrections. Baton Rouge, LA: Author.

Lundman, R.J. (1993). *Prevention and Control of Juvenile Delinquency,* Second Edition. New York, NY: Oxford University Press.

MacKenzie, D.L. (1990). "Boot Camp Prisons: Components, Evaluations, and Empirical Issues." *Federal Probation,* 54(September):44-52.

_____ (1991). "The Parole Performance of Offenders Released from Shock Incarceration (Boot Camp Prisons): A Survival Time Analysis." *Journal of Quantitative Criminology,* 7(3):213-236.

_____ (in press). "Shock Incarceration as an Alternative for Drug Offenders." In D.L. MacKenzie & C. Uchida (eds.) *Drugs and the Criminal Justice System: Evaluating Public Policy Initiatives.* Newbury Park, CA: Sage.

MacKenzie, D.L. & D. Parent (1991). "Shock Incarceration and Prison Crowding in Louisiana." *Journal of Criminal Justice,* 19(3):225-237.

_____ (1992). "Boot Camp Prison for Young Offenders" In J. Byrne, A.J. Lurigio & J. Petersilia (eds.) *Smart Sentencing: The Emergence of Intermediate Sanctions,* pp. 103-119. London: Sage Publications.

MacKenzie, D.L. & J. Shaw (1993). "The Impact of Shock Incarceration on Technical Violations and New Criminal Activities." *Justice Quarterly*, 10(3):463-487.

MacKenzie, D.L. & C. Souryal (1993). "Multi-Site Study of Shock Incarceration Process Evaluation: Final Report to the National Institute of Justice." Washington, DC: U.S. Department of Justice, National Institute of Justice. Unpublished Report.

Maher, R. & H. Dufour (1987). "Experimenting with Community Service: A Punitive Alternative to Imprisonment." *Federal Probation*, 51:22-27.

Mair, G. (1991). "The Electronic Monitoring of Offenders: Symposium Papers." *British Journal of Criminology*, 30(Autumn):451-452.

Maloney, D., D. Romig & T. Armstrong (1988). "Juvenile Probation: The Balanced Approach." *Juvenile and Family Court Journal*, 39(3).

Maxfield, M.G. & T.L. Baumer (1990). "Home Detention With Electronic Monitoring Comparing Pretrial and Postconviction Programs." *Crime & Delinquency*, 36(October):521-536.

McCarthy, B.R. (1987). *Intermediate Punishments: Intensive Supervision, Home Confinement, and Electronic Surveillance*. Monsey, NY: Criminal Justice Press.

McCarthy, B.R. & B.J. McCarthy, Jr. (1991). *Community-Based Corrections*, Second Edition. Pacific Grove, CA: Brooks-Cole.

McGarry, P. & L. Adams (1989). "Balancing Supply and Demand: A New Approach to Correctional Crowding." *The Journal of State Government*, 62(2):84-88.

McShane, M.D. & W. Krause (1993). *Community Corrections*. New York, NY: Macmillan Publishing Company.

Meehl, P.E. (1954). *Clinical vs. Statistical Prediction*. Minneapolis, MN: University of Minneapolis.

Merry, S.E. (1987). "Crowding, Conflict and Neighborhood Regulation." In I. Altman & A. Wandersman (eds.) *Neighborhood and Community Environments*, pp. 35-68. New York, NY: Plenum Press.

Minor, K.I. & D.J. Hartmann (1992). "An Evaluation of the Kalamazoo Probation Enhancement Program." *Federal Probation*, 56:30-35.

Moczydlowski, K. (1980). "Predictors of Success in a Correctional Halfway House for Youthful and Adult Offenders." *Corrective and Social Psychiatry and Journal of Behavior Technology, Methods and Therapy*, 26:59-72.

Moran, E.L., W.A. Kass & D.C. Munz (1977). "In-Program Evaluation of a Community Correctional Agency for High Risk Offenders." *Corrective and Social Psychiatry and Journal of Behavior Technology, Methods and Therapy*, 23:48-52.

Morash, M. & L. Rucker (1990). "A Critical Look at the Idea of Boot Camp as a Correctional Reform." *Crime & Delinquency*, 36(2):204-221.

Morris, N. & M. Tonry (1990). *Between Prison and Probation: Intermediate Punishments in a Rational Sentencing System*. NY: Oxford University Press.

National Council on Crime and Delinquency (1990). *Evaluation of the Florida Community Control Program*. Madison, WI.

──────── (1990). *Intensive Supervision in the United States*. Madison, WI.

──────── (1992). *Criminal Justice Sentencing Policy Statement*. San Francisco, CA: National Council on Crime and Delinquency.

Neithercutt, M.G. & D.M. Gottfredson (1974). *Caseload Size Variation and Differences in Probation/Parole Performance* (Grant No. 75-DF-99-0014). Washington, DC: National Center for Juvenile Justice.

Nellis, M. (1991). "The Electronic Monitoring of Offenders in England and Wales." *British Journal of Criminology*, 31(Spring):165-185.

New York State Department of Correctional Services and New York State Division of Parole (1991). "The Third Annual Report to the Legislature: Shock Incarceration in New York State." Unpublished report.

──────── (1992). *The Fourth Annual Report to the Legislature: Shock Incarceration— Shock Parole Supervision*. Albany, NY.

Norusis, M. (1990). *SPSS Advanced Statistics User's Guide*. Chicago, IL: SPSS Inc.

Office of Criminal Justice Coordination (1991). *Electronic Monitoring at the Youth Study Center: An Evaluation*. New Orleans, LA: Office of Criminal Justice Coordination.

O'Leary, Vincent (1985). "Reshaping Community Corrections." *Crime and Delinquency*, 31:349-366.

──────── (1987). "Probation: A System in Change." *Federal Probation*, LI(4):8-11.

Orsagh, T. & M.E. Marsden (1985). "What Works When: Rational-Choice Theory and Offender Rehabilitation." *Journal of Criminal Justice*, 13:269-277.

Osler, M.W. (1991). "Shock Incarceration: Hard Realities and Real Possibilities." *Federal Probation*, 55:34-36.

Palm Beach County, Florida Sheriff's Department (1987). "Palm Beach County's In-House Arrest Work Release Program." In B.R. McCarthy (ed.) *Intermediate Punishments: Intensive Supervision, Home Confinement and Electronic Surveillance*, pp. 181-187, Monsey, NY: Willow Tree Press, Inc.

Palmer, T. (1992). *The Re-Emergence of Correctional Intervention*. Newbury Park, CA: Sage.

Parent, D.G. (1988). *Shock Incarceration: An Overview of Existing Programs*. National Institute of Justice Research Monograph, U.S. Department of Justice. Washington, DC: U.S. Government Printing Office.

_____ (1989). "Shock Incarceration: An Overview of Existing Programs." *NIJ Issues and Practices*. Washington, DC: National Institute of Justice.

Pearson, F.S. (1987). *Research on New Jersey's Intensive Supervision Program*. Final report submitted to National Institute of Justice, U.S. Department of Justice under Grant #83-IJ-CSX-K027, Washington, DC.

Pearson, F.S. & A.G. Harper (1990). "Contingent Intermediate Sanctions: New Jersey's Intensive Supervision Program." *Crime and Delinquency*, 36:75-86.

Perkins, D.D., P. Florin, R.C. Rich, A. Wandersman & D.M. Chavis (1990). "Participation and the Social and Physical Environment of Residential Blocks: Crime and Community Context." *American Journal of Community Psychology*, 18:83-116.

Petersilia, J. (1987). *Expanding Options for Criminal Sentencing*. Santa Monica, CA: The Rand Corporation.

_____ (1991). "Evaluating Alternative Sanctions: The Case of Intensive Supervision." *Federal Sentencing Reporter*, 4(1):30-33.

Petersilia, J., J. Peterson & S. Turner (1992). "Evaluating Intensive Probation and Parole Supervision Programs: Results of a Nationwide Experiment." Unpublished Manuscript.

Petersilia, J. & S. Turner (1990). *Intensive Supervision for High-Risk Probationers: Findings from Three California Experiments*. Santa Monica, CA: The Rand Corporation.

_____ (1990). "Comparing Intensive and Regular Supervision for High-Risk Probationers: Early Results From an Experiment in California." *Crime and Delinquency* 36:87-111.

_____ (1991). "An Evaluation of Intensive Probation in California." *Journal of Criminology and Criminal Law*, 82:610-658.

_____ (1993). "Evaluating Intensive Supervision Probation/Parole: Results of a Nationwide Experiment." *Research in Brief*. Washington DC: National Institute of Justice.

Quinn, M. (1993). "'Boot Camp' at San Quentin: Pilot Program Offers Military-Style Rehabilitation." *San Francisco Chronicle,* East Bay Edition, January 19, pp. A13, A16.

Renzema, M. (1989). "Annual Monitoring Census: Progress Report." *Journal of Offender Monitoring,* 2:20-21.

_____ (1991). "Half Empty or Half Full." *Journal of Offender Monitoring,* 4:1-11.

Renzema, M. & D. Skelton (1990). "The Scope of Electronic Monitoring Today." *Journal of Offender Monitoring,* 4:6-11.

_____ (1990). "Trends in the Use of Electronic Monitoring." *Journal of Offender Monitoring,* 3(3):12-19.

Rogers, R. & A. Jolin (1989). "Electronic Monitoring: A Review of The Empirical Literature." *Journal of Contemporary Criminal Justice,* 5(3):141-152.

Rosenfeld, R. & K. Kempf (1991). "The Scope and Purposes of Corrections: Exploring Alternative Responses to Crowding." *Crime and Delinquency,* 37:481-505.

Rosenthal, C. (1989). *Opportunities in Community Corrections.* National Conference of State Legislatures, Denver, Colorado.

SAS (1985). *SAS User's Guide: Statistic Version 5 Edition.* Cary, NC: SAS Institute, Inc.

Scheff, T.J. (1992). "Three Recommendations for California Crime Control Policy." Working paper of the California Policy Seminar, Berkeley, CA.

Schoen, K. (1972). "PORT: A New Concept of Community-Based Correction." *Federal Probation,* 36:35-40.

Sechrest, D. (1989). "Prison 'Boot Camps' Do Not Measure Up." *Federal Probation,* 53(3):15-20.

Shaw, J.W. & D.L. MacKenzie (1991). "Shock Incarceration and Its Impact of the Lives of Problem Drinkers." *American Journal of Criminal Justice,* 16(1):63-96.

Skogan, W.G. & M.G. Maxfield (1981). *Coping with Crime.* Beverly Hills, CA: Sage.

Smykla, J.O. (1981). *Community-Based Corrections: Principles and Practices.* New York, NY: Macmillan.

South Carolina Department of Probation, Parole, and Pardon Services (SCDPPPS) (1989). *South Carolina Shock Probation Unit Evaluation: Qualitative and Descriptive Analysis.* Columbia, SC.

State Reorganization Commission (SRC) (1990). *An Evaluation of the Omnibus Criminal Justice Improvements Act of 1986.* Columbia, SC.

Tallahassee Democrat (1991). "Grim Times Abound in a Slash and Burn State," *Tallahassee Democrat,* February, 17, 1991.

Taylor, R.B. (1982). "The Neighborhood Physical Environment and Stress." In G.W. Evans (ed.) *Environmental Stress,* pp. 286-324. New York, NY: Cambridge University Press.

_____ (1988). *Human Territorial Functioning: An Empirical Evolutionary Perspective on Individual and Small Group Territorial Cognitions, Behaviors and Consequences.* Cambridge, England: Cambridge University Press.

Tennessee Department of Correction (1991). *Annual Report: Fiscal Year 1989-90.* Nashville, TN: Tennessee Department of Correction.

_____ (1990a). *Annual Report: Fiscal Year 1988-89.* Nashville, TN: Tennessee Department of Correction.

_____ (1990b). *Research Brief: Changes in Total Correctional Population.* Nashville, TN: Tennessee Department of Correction.

Tennessee Sentencing Commission (1990). *Criminal Justice Handbook, 1990.* Nashville, TN: Tennessee Sentencing Commission.

Thibault, E.A. & J.J. Maceri (1986). "N.Y.S. Proactive Probation Time Management." *New York State Journal of Probation and Parole*, 17:17-22.

Thoits, P.A. (1982). "Life Stress, Social Support, and Psychological Vulnerability: Epidemiological Considerations." *Journal of Community Psychology*, 10:341-362.

Tonry, M. (1990). "Stated and Latent Functions of ISP." *Crime and Delinquency*, 36:174-191.

Tonry, M. & R. Will (1988). *Intermediate Sanctions.* Preliminary Report to the National Institute of Justice. Washington, DC: National Institute of Justice.

Turner, S. & J. Petersilia (1992). "Focusing on High-Risk Parolees: An Experiment to Reduce Commitments to the Texas Department of Corrections." *Journal of Research in Crime and Delinquency*, 29:34-61.

Unger, D.G. & A. Wandersman (1985). "The Importance of Neighbors: The Social, Cognitive, and Affective Components of Neighboring." *American Journal of Community Psychology*, 13:291-300.

U.S. Department of Justice (1990). *Survey of Intermediate Sanctions.* Washington, DC: U.S. Government Printing Office.

U.S. Department of Justice, Bureau of Justice Statistics (1992). *Correctional Populations in the United States.* Washington, DC: U.S. Department of Justice, Bureau of Justice Statistics.

United States General Accounting Office (1993). *Intensive Probation Supervision: Crime-Control and Cost-Saving Effectiveness*. Washington, DC: Author.

Vaughn, J.B. (1987). "Planning for Change: The Use of Electronic Monitoring as a Correctional Alternative." In B.R. McCarthy (ed.) *Intermediate Punishments: Intensive Supervision, Home Confinement and Electronic Surveillance*, pp. 153-168, Monsey, NY: Willow Tree Press, Inc.

_____ (1989). "A Survey of Juvenile Electronic Monitoring and Home Confinement Programs." *Juvenile & Family Court Journal*, 40:1-36.

_____ (1991). "Use of Electronic Monitoring With Juvenile Intensive Supervision Programs," pp. 189-209. In T. Armstrong (ed.) *Intensive Supervision With High-risk Youths*. Monsey, NY: Criminal Justice Press.

Von Hirsch, A. (1976). *Doing Justice: The Choice of Punishments*. New York, NY: Hill and Wang.

Wiedemann, S. & J.R. Anderson (1985). "A Conceptual Framework for Residential Satisfaction." In I. Altman & C.M. Werner (eds.) *Home Environments*, pp. 153-182. New York, NY: Plenum Press.

Weisheit, R. (1992). "Patterns of Female Crime." In R.G. Culbertson and R. Weisheit (eds.) *Order Under Law*, Fourth Edition, pp. 59-72, Prospect Heights, IL: Waveland Press.

White House (1989). National Drug Control Strategy. Washington, DC: U.S. Government Printing Office.

Wilbanks, W. (1987). *The Myth of a Racist Criminal Justice System*. Monterey, CA: Brooks/Cole Publishing Company.

Wolfgang, M., R. Figlio & T. Sellin (1972). *Delinquency in a Birth Cohort*. Chicago, IL: University of Chicago Press.

INDEX

About the Authors

Timothy R. Brehm is a Community Corrections Specialist with the North Dakota Division of Parole and Probation. He graduated in 1984 from Valley City State University with a bachelor's degree in human resources administration and management.

Michael P. Brown is an Assistant Professor in the Department of Criminal Justice and Criminology at Ball State University. He received his Ph.D. in sociology from Western Michigan University in 1992. Brown's current research interests include intermediate sanctions, juvenile justice, and decisionmaking.

Thomas C. Castellano is an Associate Professor in the Center for the Study of Crime, Delinquency, and Corrections at Southern Illinois University at Carbondale. He received his Ph.D. in criminal justice from SUNY at Albany in 1986. Castellano's current research projects include an analysis of drug treatment programming in shock incarceration programs and an evaluation of parole reform in Illinois.

Ernest L. Cowles is the Director of the Center for Legal Studies and an Associate Professor at Sangamon State University in Springfield, Illinois. In addition to ongoing corrections research, he is currently involved in an evaluation of multijurisdictional drug task forces. Cowles received his Ph.D. from Florida State University in 1981.

Paul C. Friday is an Professor and Chair of Criminal Justice at the University of North Carolina—Charlotte. He is active in social policy issues and is currently assessing court processes, alternative sanctions and conducting research linking medical and legal data on gunshot wounds. Friday's specialty area is comparative juvenile delinquency.

Betsy Fulton is the Principal Investigator for the American Probation and Parole Association (APPA) where she manages the activities of a national grant project, Technical Assistance and Training for Intensive Supervision

Programs. Those activities include research, training, and technical assistance. She previously developed curricula and provided training and technical assistance to probation and parole agencies for a national grant, Drug Testing throughout the Criminal Justice System: Probation and Parole Component. Before joining the staff of APPA, Fulton served as Intensive Supervision Program Coordinator in Greene County, Ohio. She has a bachelor's degree in sociology from Miami University—Oxford, Ohio, and a master's degree in applied behavioral science from Wright State University in Dayton, Ohio.

Laura A. Gransky received her master's degree in criminal justice from Southern Illinois University at Carbondale in 1993. She is currently employed as a legal research associate at the Center for Legal Studies at Sangamon State University. Gransky's major areas of interest are in the planning, implementation, and evaluation of correctional programs.

Stephen Haas is a doctoral student in the Department of Criminal Justice at the University of Cincinnati. He completed his undergraduate work in political science at Ohio State University and his M.S. in criminal justice at the University of Cincinnati. Haas' research interests are in corrections.

Richard M. Hoekstra is the Intensive Programs Coordinator with the North Dakota Division of Parole and Probation. He graduated in 1980 from Moorhead State University with a B.A. in criminal justice.

Edward J. Latessa is a Professor and the Head of the Department of Criminal Justice at the University of Cincinnati. He received his Ph.D. in Public Administration from Ohio State University in 1979. Latessa has written extensively in the area of community-based corrections and treatment and is co-author of *Probation and Parole in America, Introduction to Criminal Justice Research Methods, and Statistical Applications in Criminal Justice*. He is also past president of the Academy of Criminal Justice Sciences. Latessa's research interests are in intensive supervision, offender rehabilitation, and methods of evaluating criminal justice interventions.

Doris Layton Mackenzie is a Research Scholar in the Department of Criminal Justice and Criminology at the University of Maryland. Prior to joining the Maryland faculty, she was Associate Professor at Louisiana State University with joint appointments in criminal justice and experimental statistics. She has published papers in the areas of inmate adjustment, recidivism, prison crowding, and classification, and is co-editor of two books, *The American Prison: Issues in Research Policy* and *Measuring Crime: Large-Scale, Long Range Efforts*. Currently, Mackenzie is director of a multi-site study of shock incarceration examining eight shock incarceration programs.

Larry S. Miller is a Professor in the Department of Criminal Justice and Criminology at East Tennessee State University. His recent research has concerned intensive probation and police issues. Miller is the author of numerous articles and textbooks including *Sansone's Police Photography*, Third Edition (Anderson Publishing Co., 1993).

Laura B. Myers is an Assistant Professor in the College of Criminal Justice at Sam Houston State University. Her current research interests include jury decisionmaking in capital cases and sentencing issues.

Barry J. Nidorf is the Chief Probation Officer in Los Angeles County. He received his master's degree in public administration from the University of Southern California in 1976. Nidorf is recognized internationally as an expert in the field of adult and juvenile probation and has served as a member of the National Institute of Corrections Advisory Board.

Robert L. Polakow is the Director of Program Development and Evaluation at Los Angeles County Probation Department. He received his master's degree in psychology from California State University, Northridge, in 1974. He has worked for the Los Angeles County Probation Department for more than 25 years and published extensively in the field of corrections.

Paige H. Ralph is an Assistant Professor of criminal justice at Lake Superior State University. She received her Ph.D. in criminal justice from Sam Houston State University in 1992. In addition to community corrections, Ralph's research interests include prison violence, inmate gangs, and sentencing disparity.

Sudipto Roy is an Assistant Professor in the Department of Criminology at Indiana State University. He received his Ph.D. in sociology from Western Michigan University in 1990. Roy's research interests include victimology, restitution, and electronic surveillance.

Claire Souryal is a doctoral student in the Department of Criminal Justice and Criminology at the University of Maryland. She is currently working as a research associate on a multi-site study of eight shock incarceration programs directed by Doris Layton Mackenzie.

Susan Stone is a Research Associate with the American Probation and Parole Association (APPA) where she manages the Offender Supervision and Victim Restitution Project sponsored by the Office for Victims of Crime. She previously worked as Research Assistant on the Technical Assistance and Training for Intensive Supervision Programs sponsored by the Bureau of Justice Assistance. Stone has a master's degree in public administration from the University of Kentucky and is a former juvenile probation officer.

Robert A. Wertkin is a Professor and the Director of the School of Social Work at Western Michigan University. He is a specialist on child welfare, organizational structure, institutional violence, and program evaluation. Wertkin's recent works include analysis of public child welfare services, social work education; and communication dynamics, supervision, and management in public agencies.

John T. Whitehead is an Associate Professor in the Department of Criminal Justice and Criminology at East Tennessee State University. His recent research has concerned intensive probation and school victimization. Whitehead is co-author (with Steven P. Lab) of *Juvenile Justice: An Introduction* (Anderson Publishing Co., 1990), and is co-author (with Larry S. Miller) of *Criminal Justic Statistics* (Anderson Publishing Co., in press).

Sheldon X. Zhang is an Assistant Professor in the Department of Sociology at California State University, San Marcos. He received his Ph.D. from University of Southern California in 1993. Previously, he worked as a researcher for Los Angeles County Probation Department. His major research interests include community corrections, social control issues in juvenile delinquency, and ethnic youth offenders.

About the Editors

William L. Selke received his Ph.D. from Michigan State University. He is an Associate Professor of criminal justice at Indiana University. His primary teaching and research interests include prison administration, correctional reform, and community corrections. He has just published *Prisons in Crisis.*

John Ortiz Smykla is Professor and Chairperson of criminal justice at the University of Alabama. He received his Ph.D. from Michigan State University. His teaching and research interests focus on Latin American criminal justice, military reconstruction and southern law enforcement, sexually integrated prisons, and community corrections. He is author of *Cocorrections: A Case Study of a Coed Federal Prison, Community-Based Corrections, Probation and Parole*, and editor of *Coed Prison.*